42 Things I Wish I Had Known When I Started to Trade Stocks, Forex, CFD

Written by *Andrei Puscaragiu*

An individual trader since 2005, trying to obtain positive returns on his trades, like many others out there

Trading is hard, and it is *not* suitable for everyone.

+ Are you fully aware of **all the risks that arise** from trading?

+ Do you understand the **unwritten rules** of the financial markets?

+ Do you get that you **are on your own in a combat** with other individual traders and investors, investments funds, hedge funds, banks, and other market participants?

+ Do you realize that one of the financial market's rules is **"eat or be eaten"**?

You, and only you, are responsible for taking care of your hard-earned money.

Dear reader,

Perhaps you are interested in finding more about trading. Or maybe you have been trading for a while, and you want to learn more from other traders' experience. By reading this book you can understand how trading may look and feel like for an ordinary individual trader. You may also learn from the many mistakes I have made over the years. I am sure that a lot of other traders have made the same mistakes and many more will continue to do so in the future.

The purpose of this miniguide is *not* to sell you the idea of trading or investing. The goal of this miniguide is *not* to convince you that trading is easy (because it's not!). Nor is it to sell you a "magic recipe," so "simple" and "easy" that even a monkey can apply it to become a profitable trader.

You will find inside the most important forty-two things I have learned the hard way, losing my own money. I have to admit that many times I made poor trading decisions: letting fear or greed take over, ignoring my trading rules, buying high and selling low.

Before going any further, please allow me to briefly introduce myself. My name is Andrei. I have been trading since 2005, mainly stocks. I also traded on margin contracts for difference (CFDs) on currencies (forex), indices, and commodities. During the years I experienced both very good and very bad times: I know how it feels to win $1,000 in two to three days; I know how it feels to lose $1,000 in a single day. I have a background in finance. I am not a full-time trader. Over the years, I had several jobs in the financial trading industry: I worked as a stock broker, sales/business developer, and marketer.

I wrote this miniguide because I wish I had read a similar one when I started to trade the financial markets. If I had known then what I know today, it would have helped me achieve better results.

    If you decide to read it, I hope you will find it useful.
Andrei Puscaragiu

Table of Contents

Part 1: The WHY, the WHAT and the WHO

Why Did I Write This Miniguide, and Who Should Read It?

What This Miniguide Isn't About

Why Should You Read the Miniguide, and What's in It for You?

About the Author

Why Did I Write This Miniguide, and Who Should Read It?

I wrote this miniguide because I wish I had read a similar one before placing my first trade on the market. I would have been better prepared for what followed once I decided to start trading. If I had known then what I know today, it would have helped me make better decisions and achieve better results.

Each day, new traders and investors start to ride the market roller coaster. Armed with enthusiasm and hope, they begin their quest for (big) profits. Unfortunately, for some of them the ride turns out to be a nightmare, and they end up losing (a lot of) money.

I wrote this miniguide for them—the ordinary, individual traders. They are not professional traders; maybe they don't even have a background in economics, finance, or investing. They are not full-time traders, as they also have another occupation. They may be doctors, teachers, lawyers, bankers, accountants, engineers, drivers, sales agents, managers, business owners—you name it—young or old, male or female, trading with $500, $5,000, or $50,000.

There are so many things that differentiate one trader from another. Still, they have something in common: they are all willing to risk their hard-earned money and trade the markets for profits. They may trade different financial instruments—stocks, indices, commodities, currencies, and so forth—but they all try to speculate the short-term and/or medium-term price fluctuations.

Do you find yourself fitting the above description? If yes, then I wrote this miniguide for you. If you are currently considering starting trading or have been trading for a while but could not manage it profitably, this miniguide is for you.

On understanding how trading may look and feel like, you may decide to be more cautious. Learning from the (costly) mistakes I made, you may learn to avoid them.

Let's see in more detail what this miniguide is and isn't about.

What This Miniguide Isn't About

There are a lot of books trying to sell the idea that trading is simple and easy, so simple and easy that even a monkey can do it. So if a monkey can do it, you can do it too!

Let me assure you that this miniguide is nothing like that. On the contrary, it may make you think twice about trading the financial markets.

1. The purpose of this miniguide is *not* to sell you the idea of trading or investing.

2. The goal of this miniguide is *not* to convince you that trading is easy (because it's not!).

3. This is *not* a book selling "secret recipes" or anything else that is "guaranteed" to help you boost your winnings overnight. When you trade the markets, the only guarantee is that nothing is 100 percent certain.

4. You will *not* find inside "simple" techniques that will show you "easy" ways to become a "successful" trader overnight.

There are of course many solid books written by experts, that can help you learn the theoretical aspects from A to Z: types of assets, assets valuation, asset allocation, fundamental analysis, technical analysis, risk management, and so forth. You get the point. Having solid knowledge about the theory of investing and trading is necessary for success (but not sufficient).

5. This miniguide is not about the theoretical stuff.

So why should you read this miniguide? What is it about, and what's in it for you?

Why Should You Read the Miniguide, and What's in It for You?

1. If you are about to start trading or if you have already started, I believe that you will make some, most, or even all of the mistakes other traders (just like you) already made. You can choose to ignore them, hoping that you are lucky enough to avoid them. Please understand that some lessons can prove to be quite costly! Or you can choose to pay attention at other people's experiences and increase your awareness regarding the possible risks related to trading.

2. By reading the miniguide, you will better understand the invisible traps associated with trading. No, I am not just talking about the risk of losing money, which is quite obvious. To get my point through, here are just few examples of the traps:

+ the trap in which you can fall into when you have a good momentum, when your trades are profitable, and you start feeling invincible

+ the urge to get back in the game after you suffer a significant loss

+ the possibility that you will become addicted to trading: the feelings of power and invincibility when you cash out a profitable trade, the euphoria of winning money—all these will trigger the craving to trade more and more, even though there are no clear investment opportunities in the market

+ the risk of losing interest in everything around you when you go through a rough patch and your losses pile up: you feel drained of energy; it's never been harder to do your job and chores; you are not in the mood to spend time with your family or grab a beer with your friends; you are not able to enjoy the taste of food; you do not have the mind-set to enjoy walking in the park, reading a book, or watching a movie or a football game. Everything seems pointless.

3. You will learn from the ups and downs of an individual trader (let's call him Andrei...yes, that's me!). He was captivated by the financial markets' mirage. Sometimes he won, and sometimes he lost, but he always tried to learn from his mistakes. Some of them were costly, as many times he acted foolishly; he was buying because he was greedy or selling because he was fearful. You will get all these lessons for free.

You may not relate to everything I discuss in the miniguide. Choose the ideas that have meaning for you, analyze them, dig deeper, and see how you can use them to better fit your purposes. In the end, take care of your money; it's your responsibility.

About the Author

My name is Andrei, and I have been trading since 2005. I am an individual trader, trying to obtain positive returns on my trades, like many other traders out there.

I have a background in finance. I am not a full-time trader. Over the years, I had several jobs in the financial trading industry: I worked as a stock broker, sales/business developer, and marketer.

I have been trading mainly stocks. I also have experience in trading on margin futures contracts and CFDs on currencies (forex), indices, and commodities.

So far I had only traded on short and medium terms, meaning that I usually kept my open positions for few days, weeks, and sometimes even months. I was not the "buy and hold" kind of guy with long-term investment approach (holding the positions for years).

I use both fundamental and technical analysis in combination with risk management and investment psychology.

During the years I experienced both very good and very bad times: I know how it feels to win $1,000 in two to three days; I know how it feels to lose $1,000 in a single day.

The 2007–2009 financial crisis hit me pretty hard and left me with some scars. I saw the stock market crash with my own eyes, live, day by day, for almost a year and a half. Blood, fear, recession, painful moments—the time felt like it was the end of the world, the end of everything, but somehow I managed to survive. I was seriously "wounded," no doubt about it, but I was still in the game. This is why I became more risk averse and more cautious.

For example, while writing this paragraph, I keep more than 85 percent of my savings in safe, low interest rate bank deposits, while less than 15 percent of my money is in my trading account in search of higher (potential) returns Why 15 percent? Because this is the maximum level I am willing to risk in the market.

Currently, I prefer trading on longer time frames, and my goal is to constantly generate positive returns.

That's about it. Let's start now with the things I wish I knew before placing my first trade. Are you ready?

Part 2: Unwritten Laws, Invisible Risks, and Few Other Things You Need to Know

#1 Eat or Be Eaten

#2 Four Basic (and Obvious) Things Every Trader Should Know

#3 You Are Your Worst Enemy

#4 When You Trade the Markets, You Are at War with Your Emotions: Fear and Greed Are Plotting Against You

#5 If You Are Not a Fan of Discipline and Self-Control, Your Life as a Trader Will Be Difficult

Let's See How Being a Trader Might Look and Feel Like

Let's Draw Some Conclusions

#1 Eat or Be Eaten

When you trade the markets, you compete with other participants: individual traders and investors, investment funds, hedge funds, banks, asset management companies, etc., and you are on your own. It's your own responsibility to take care of your money. And avoid "being eaten" by others.

There are situations when, for some to win, others have to lose or at least incur an opportunity cost. Let's take a look at this idea.

At any given moment, for a specific financial instrument, there are two types of market participants: the buyers and the sellers. Each participant takes his decision for his own reasons and according to his own strategy. For example, one can buy a long-term investment, another can sell to obtain the cash he or she needs for a different trade, while another can just try to speculate and make a profit from the short-term price movement (by either buying or selling).

I think it's safe to say that, at a given moment, for a specific financial instrument, you can find among all the buyers and sellers, at least one buyer and one seller whose goal is to speculate the short-term price fluctuation. Basically, they bet against each other; once the price moves either up or down, one of them is right, and the other is wrong. This means that one wins, while the other loses or at least incurs an opportunity cost.

Let's take a simple example. Trader A and trader B are both active traders, trading the markets to speculate the price fluctuations. Financial instrument XYZ is currently traded at $10.

Trader A expects the price of XYZ to go up, so she wants to buy. Trader B bought XYZ some time ago at $8, and he wants to take his profits off the table, because he believes the price will slide. Trader A buys XYZ at $10, and trader B sells XYZ at $10.

Scenario 1: XYZ slides to $9.

If trader A sells at $9, she will have a loss.

If she does not sell and the price recovers, she will have an opportunity cost: instead of buying at $10, she could have bought at $9.

Scenario 2: XYZ goes up to $11.

Trader A can sell and make a profit.

Trader B incurred an opportunity cost. He has a profit indeed (he bought at $8 and sold at $10), but his profit would have been bigger if he had waited and sold at $11.

In this example, one trader will win, while the other will lose or will at least incur an opportunity cost (meaning that he will have less profit than he could have obtained).

Let's take another example. If we analyze the historical chart for a specific financial instrument, we can identify the lows and the highs for different downtrends and uptrends. Now think about the low of a downtrend. Near the low, there were market participants that bought at very good prices. But for them to buy, it was necessary for others to sell near the low because for each trade you need a buyer and a seller, right? It is similar for the high of an uptrend. Near the high, there were market participants that sold at very good prices, but for them to sell, it was necessary for others to buy near the high.

In this example, it is obvious that for some traders to buy low, others have to sell low, and for some traders to sell high, others have to buy high. That's just the way it is.

I am not saying that financial markets are a zero-sum game. My point is that there are situations when, for some to win, others have to lose or at least to incur an opportunity cost.

You need to be aware of this and avoid being eaten by others.

#2 Four Basic (and Obvious) Things Every Trader Should Know

Trading is risky.

Do you understand that you can lose money? Can you accept this risk?

Let's do an exercise. Imagine that you lost your wallet, and you had only $500 cash in it (no IDs, no cards, just cash). How would you feel, and how would you react? Would you be sad and depressed for days, even weeks? Or would you easily get over it?

If the thought of losing $500, $100, or even $50 makes you anxious, if you cannot accept the possibility of losing money, then trading may not be suitable for you.

Trading is *not* easy.

If you think that you just need to open a trading account, read some news, find few tips, and then follow your gut to "buy low and sell high," well, you are so wrong. Trading is hard. It requires

+ solid knowledge—fundamental and technical analysis—so that you (try to) predict how prices might move;

+ a solid risk management system so that you (try to) control and limit the losses when your forecasts are not correct;

+ a lot of practice so that you can develop, test, and improve your trading skills and systems;

+ self-discipline so that you (try to) respect your trading rules and not let your feelings and emotions take over; and

+ time, not only to obtain the knowledge and experience but also for the trading itself (to monitor the news and markets, to make your research, to decide the proper timing for opening and closing your trades).

And even so, there are no guarantees for success.

Trading and investing are two different things.

A trader's goal is to speculate the short- and/or medium-term price fluctuations. He can keep his open positions for minutes, hours, days, or even weeks. An investor has a buy-and-hold approach, and the time frame for his investments ranges from months to years.

Trading is more challenging than investing, because it requires more complex trading systems and risk management strategies, more precise timing for the execution of the trades (when to buy and when to sell), greater self-control, an increased ability to manage your emotions, more available time, and stronger ability to cope with stress.

The final goal for a trader is to generate returns that significantly outperform the buy-and-hold approach. (This may or may not happen.)

How does a trader try to generate profits?

"Buy low and sell high": If you expect the price to go up, you buy. If your forecast is correct, you will sell at a higher price, and you will win. If not, you will lose because you will sell at a lower price.

"Sell high and buy low": If you anticipate the price to go down, you can sell short. This means that you sell something you do not have, hoping to buy it later at a lower price. If you are correct and the price declines, you will buy at a lower price, and you will make a profit. If you are wrong and the price moves up, you will buy at a higher price, and you will lose. (We will cover short selling—both the benefits and the risks—later on.)

#3 You Are Your Worst Enemy

We hear this thing so often, and it has become some sort of stereotype. Stereotype or not, it is also true when you trade the markets. When you generate profits, you are responsible for this. When you lose money, it is hard to avoid the trap of finding excuses and blaming the market for being irrational or foolish. But at the end of the day, you, and only you, are responsible for the results of your trades.

Here are just few examples of how you can be your worst enemy when you start to ride the market roller coaster:

+ You invest borrowed money.

+ You invest money whose possible loss can affect your financial stability.

+ You have a big desire to win a lot of money fast. Therefore you allow your greed to take control of your trading decisions.

+ In high-pressure moments, when it's most needed to stay calm and rational, you let your fear take over, which usually leads to foolish and rash decisions.

+ You have a gambling problem, and you decide to "diversify" your gambling activities with trading.

+ Although you are not addicted to gambling, you treat trading like gambling, and you decide to try your luck with financial bets.

#4 When You Trade the Markets, You Are at War with Your Emotions: Fear and Greed Are Plotting Against You

When you trade the markets, it's all about winning or losing money. It is easy to understand why Greed and Fear prowl around you, trying to persuade you to give them control over your decisions. Maybe Fear sits on your left shoulder, and Greed sits on the right one. (Or the other way around, it can be different from one trader to another.) There is no more room left for your guardian angel (the one in charge with your financial well-being). You are on your own.

Imagine a trader who bought a stock because he expected the price to go up. If the market moves against him, and he starts losing money, at first he becomes a little bit anxious. As the price continues to slide, and the loss gets bigger and bigger, Fear starts to prowl around him. The thought that the price may further decline, melting down his account, is terrifying. He is stressed and concerned, wondering what he should do. Should he sell the stock? What if the price recovers? Should he wait? What if the price keeps falling? Faced with such a psychological torture, the trader decides few days later to close his position, and he sells the stock with a loss.

I am not saying that using a stop-loss order is a bad thing! This is actually recommended and necessary. However, the decision to close a losing trade should be a rational one based on analyzing the current context of the market, the fundamentals, and the technical aspects of the stock. But a trader who allows his fear to take over, closes his losing trade just because he can no longer stand the psychological torture; the anxiety, uncertainty, stress, and panic are too overwhelming.

Greed has a similar effect on our trading decisions. Imagine a trader who discovered a (possible) trading opportunity. He expects XYZ to go up 20–30 percent during the next few weeks, and he wants to buy now. His only question is how much he should invest. Although one of his trading rules is to *never* place a trade bigger than 20 percent of his account, he currently considers buying XYZ with at least 50 percent of his money. He is willing to bend the rules, just this one time so that he can fully maximize this hot opportunity. He even projects different scenarios: if he invests $10,000, he might win $2,000–3,000; if he buys with $15,000, his profit might be $3,000–4,500. That's a lot of money! Should he invest even more? He is gripped by greed, and he can no longer be rational.

If he is lucky, his forecast will be correct, and he will win. What about the next time when he will decide once more to bend the rules "just this one time"? You need to understand that luck is temporary; you can't count on it. What you can count on is a solid trading system based on clear rules. But you need to stick to your plan.

The good news is that you can win the battles against Fear and Greed. It's not easy, but it's possible. Be calm. Analyze facts and events with an objective mind. Have a set of clear rules and act accordingly.

#5 If You Are Not a Fan of Discipline and Self-Control, Your Life as a Trader Will Be Difficult

If you want to stand a chance when you trade the markets, you need to be a disciplined trader. Self-control is mandatory if you want to win the "battle of the titans" (between you and your emotions).

What can you do to become a disciplined trader?

Step 1: Establish a set of clear rules that will help you in the process of making trading decisions. Let's see some examples:

+ I will deposit in my trading account maximum 10 percent of my savings.

+ Before placing a new trade, I have to identify the stop-loss and take-profit levels.

+ If the risk-reward ratio is below 1:2, I will not enter the trade.

+ In any given trade, I will not risk more than 15 percent from the amount I have in my trading account.

+ In any given trade, I am willing to accept a loss of maximum 5 percent from the value of the trade.

+ If I suffer a loss bigger than $500, I will take a break from trading for two days.

Step two: Stick to your rules.

There will be moments when you will be tempted to ignore them. "Just this once" is what you will tell yourself the first time you will break the rules. You need to be aware that breaking the rules once creates a dangerous precedent: it will make it easier for you to skip them for a second time, for a third time, and so on.

Soon, the rules will remain just some words on a piece of paper, and you will be just another trader who lacks discipline.

And usually, a trader without discipline and self-control ends up losing his money.

Let's See How Being a Trader Might Look and Feel Like

Let's say that your savings are in amount of $50,000. You do not feel comfortable trading the markets with more than 20 percent of your money. You are aware that irrational decisions are usually made when emotions take over, and you understand that you can reduce this risk by not trading with more than $10,000, at least for now. So you open a trading account, and you deposit $10,000.

You currently do not have a clear rule about how much money to put in a single trade. In general, you go with 5–30 percent of your account based on how confident you are in your forecast. Only one time, about three months ago, you invested around 45 percent of your account in one stock. While you kept the position, the level of stress and anxiety increased a lot, because you were not comfortable having such a big exposure on one stock. At one point, when the price started to move against you and your loss got bigger and bigger, you experienced an emotional roller coaster: the fear, the worries, the sleepless nights. You felt crushed by the pressure. You even thought to close the trade just because you could not take it anymore. Fortunately, you did not give in to fear; you reassessed your trade and concluded that eventually the price would go higher, which was exactly what happened. In the end, you managed to sell the stock with a nice profit. Despite the fact that you made a profit, you swore you would never again take risks that are well above your comfort zone.

One day, you discover the stock XYZ that seems to be a good trading opportunity. You make a detailed research using both the fundamental and the technical analysis. You conclude that XYZ can be a gold mine: you forecast an upside potential between

50 and 70 percent. You are very confident in your prediction, and you are determined to buy. The only question is: how much money should you invest?

A voice in your head tells you to go all in. The voice whispers different scenarios and numbers: "If you invest all the money from your account—$10,000—and the stock goes up at least 50 percent, you will make a profit of $5,000. Now that's a lot of money!"

It seems you forgot the emotional roller coaster you experienced not long time ago and the oath you took then. The desire to take full advantage of this (possible) one time opportunity makes you blind: you don't realize that the voice in your head (projecting numbers and profits) is actually your Greed.

So you buy XYZ for $10,000. (Meanwhile, Greed sits comfortably on your left shoulder and opens a bottle of champagne, celebrating the victory.)

The timing is perfect: during the next two weeks, the price goes up 20 percent, and you already have a profit of $2,000. You are proud of your decision, and you congratulate yourself for having the guts to act. You expect XYZ to gain another 25–40 percent.

Suddenly, a new idea pops into your head: most probably, you will not find very soon a new gold mine like XYZ, so you should really take advantage of this "safe bet." Why not transfer more money from your savings account to your trading account? Without realizing it, the voice in your head starts whispering again: "If you transfer $15,000 to buy more XYZ, and the price gains 30 percent (which is highly possible), your total profit will be an incredible $10,100!"

For less than five seconds, you become aware of your rule: do not trade on the market with more than 20 percent of your money. In this moment, you have a total of $52,000, meaning that you should have in your trading account no more than $10,400. So you should actually decrease your exposure to risky assets, and withdraw $1,600 from the trading account. In the same time, the idea of betting a huge amount of money on a single stock makes you feel a weird sensation in your stomach: it's that intense feeling you have when you are about to do something you know you should not do.

The voice in your head feels that it might lose the battle, so it starts whispering again: "You had the guts before, you acted on it, and it turned out OK. You need to maximize the profits on this kind of rare opportunities. If you transfer more money now, you can cash out later more than $10,000 in profit. It's your net salary for more than two months! It's what you can save in eight months!"

Greed just won another battle: you decide to ignore the weird sensation in your stomach and break your rule, just this one time. You transfer $15,000 into your trading account, and buy more XYZ stocks. You now have a long position of $27,000. (Greed is ecstatic. The job is done.)

You now sit comfortably in your chair, ready (hoping) to see how the price moves in your favor. You do not have a clear plan for the negative scenario in case the price declines. You just make a quick calculation: if the price moves down around 7.4 percent, you will lose only the $2,000 profit. You feel safe, because you can actually lose from your initial funds only if the price loses more than 8 percent. And you don't think this is possible.

But one thing the market teaches a trader is to never say never. Despite your expectations, XYZ starts to fall, and during the next two weeks, the stock is down 7 percent. You have no idea what is going on or why the stock is being aggressively sold. Your profit is slashed: you now have less than $150 profit.

The worst thing is that you have no idea how to react. What should you do now? Should you sell the stock? But what if the price starts to recover? Should you hold your long position? But what if the price declines further? You feel helpless. (You are so overwhelmed by all these thoughts that it's impossible to hear Greed laughing.)

You are still anchored in your desire for a big profit. You hope that somehow the price will move up. You decide to stick with your initial plan. Unfortunately, when trading the markets, hope and reality often prove to be two different concepts. During the next three weeks, XYZ slides another 10 percent.

The last couple of weeks were awfully painful. As the stock got hammered, the emotional roller coaster increased its speed. You became increasingly anxious and stressed, you slept less, and there were nights when you could not sleep at all because of the worries. You lost your focus at work, and your family noticed there is something wrong with you, as you became bitter.

In just few weeks, the value of your trading account decreased from a maximum value of $27,000 to $22,600. Not only you lost the entire profit you initially had on XYZ, but you also lost $2,400 from your initial funds. It's what you can save in two months. You are desperate. You are tired. You would like to speak with somebody about this to ease the pain, but you can't; you feel like a big failure. You cannot handle the pressure anymore, so you decide to sell.

(While you fill in the fields of the Sell Order window, Greed—sitting on your left shoulder—and Fear—sitting on your right shoulder—are opening a bottle of champagne, congratulating themselves for their enormous success—your failure.)

After you sold your XYZ stocks, you decide to take a break. During the next few days, you resist the urge to log in to your trading account, but the desire to recover your money grows bigger and bigger. You fell off the stock market roller coaster; this is true. But the temptation to go for another ride is powerful, and you can no longer resist: you open your trading account, looking for opportunities that can make you money fast. Unfortunately, you do not realize that you are affected by your recent loss. You are "blinded," and you cannot identify the real opportunities. For few days, you trade like a crazy person, and you lose another $2,000.

You now understand it's time to get off the stock market roller coaster to analyze what happened, draw the conclusions, and learn the lessons that need to be learned.

Let's Draw Some Conclusions

Discipline and self-control are necessary (but not sufficient) for your success as a trader. In order to become a disciplined trader, you need to design a clear set of rules. You must understand that there is no one-size-fits-all approach. Each trader has to define his own rules. The goal: to remove emotions (as much as possible) from the decision-making process.

It seems simple but it's not. Creating an efficient set of rules takes time and practice, and it requires a solid and coherent analysis of our past decisions and patterns. We can improve our chances for success only if we understand why we lost money on a trade, what mistake we made, what was the trigger for that mistake, and so on. Again it seems simple but it's not.

Creating the rules is only the first step. The second step is sticking to the plan. The third step is constantly improving the rules based on the findings from the analysis of our past decisions. Repeating the cycle is the fourth step.

It is important not to bend the rules while you are "in the game." Do not use the excuse of "improving the rules" just to avoid them whenever greed and fear are pushing you to act irrational. Otherwise the only one that will get fooled will be you.

Part 3: Trading, Gambling, and Addiction

#6 Do You Have a Gambling Problem? Trading the Markets Can Be Lethal to You

#7 How to Decrease the Risk to Start Treating Trading like Gambling?

#8 You Can Become Addicted to Trading

#6 Do You Have a Gambling Problem? Trading the Markets Can Be Lethal to You

There are "traders" that have a big problem: they are addicted to gambling. They are fascinated by the idea of making a lot of money overnight. They have tested different forms of gambling: online betting, casinos, slot machines, poker, you name it. Most of them are net losers, meaning that overall they lost (much) more than they won. And yet, they continue to believe and hope that the next bet will bring them the big prize, the jackpot.

Somehow they discovered financial trading. From their perspective, it's quite simple to bet with financial products: the price can either go up or down. They believe it's a fifty-fifty shot, and they like the odds. Fundamental analysis, technical analysis, risk management…what the heck are those? They only trust their intuition!

But the market does not care about your intuition. At any given moment, the chances for the price of a financial instrument to go either up or down are almost never fifty-fifty. Sophisticated investors (such as investment funds) use complicated mathematical models to calculate the statistical probabilities of how the price might move. These results might show that the odds are, for example, 45/55 or 75/25 or whatever. Of course, the results and the forecasts are not 100 percent accurate, and they might even prove to be wrong. This is not magic. Still it's so much more solid than: "I have a good feeling about this stock."

If you know you have a problem with gambling, and you consider trying your luck on the markets, don't do it! Trading should not be treated like gambling. If you bet on financial products, you might win some bets, but most probably on the long run, you will end up being a net loser.

#7 How to Decrease the Risk to Start Treating Trading like Gambling?

If you do not have a problem with gambling, that's great! However, you need to be aware of this potential trap: there may be moments when you are tempted to treat trading like gambling.

You may think, "I see that XYZ gained more than 40 percent in the last couple of weeks. I did not follow this stock so far, I do not have any information about it, but I feel tempted to buy it. I don't want to put a lot of money in it…I can put a few hundred dollars, maybe a thousand, just this once…I have a gut feeling that the price can go up another 20 percent. If I am right, I will make some easy money. If not…at least I will have some fun."

What do you say, does it sound like gamble? It does to me. The risk derives from the possibility that once you place one small bet, you will do it again and again. Before you know it, "just this once" turns into a bad habit: you are no longer trading, you are betting on financial products. You are no longer a trader; you are a gambler.

So what can you do if you observe that you have the tendency to place small bets on the market? Create this rule: "Never place a trade without having the proper fundamental and technical arguments to support it or 'zero tolerance' for betting on the market."

#8 You Can Become Addicted to Trading

I guess you agree that trading the markets can easily turn into an addiction for those that have an inclination toward gambling. They already have the "bad habit" in their blood, and by trading they keep on "feeding" it, fueled by the thrills and emotions of being in the game, the strong desire to make money easy and fast, the adrenaline of winning, the chase and the hope for the big jackpot.

What about the lucky ones that do not have an inclination toward gambling, the traders that usually take calculated decisions based on research, data, and facts? Can they become addicted to trading? I believe they too can face this risk, especially when they go through a rough patch when their decisions prove to be uninspired, and they lose money.

Difficult times, when you go from one loss to another, are quite dangerous. Because you feel the urge to recover your losses, you allocate more time than before to read the news, analyze the markets, and find new possible opportunities. During your day job, you feel distracted, your productivity goes down, and you become disengaged. You check your trading account ten times more often to be sure you don't miss out on anything. You spend a lot less time with your family and friends. You go to bed thinking about some trading idea. The first thing you do when you wake up in the morning is to check the markets. If it was possible, you would take a break from your regular life (job, chores, family, and so on), and you would focus solely on trading. Does it sound like an addiction? Yep!

So what should you do? Take a step back, and breathe.
Instead of feeding the urge to be connected with the markets all the time, you should consider unplugging yourself and

taking a break from trading and following the markets. When you regain your control, you can get back in the game.

(Before you do so, you need to add stop-loss and take-profit orders for your open positions. This helps you protect your account during your "no trading" period. Also you have no excuses to break your rules and log in to your trading account to check if everything is OK.)

Part 4: Beginner's Luck and Being the Right Person in the Right place at the Right Time

#9 What's the Worst Possible Start for You as a Trader? To Make a Profit on Your Very First Trade

#10 Do You Succeed in Making Money by Speculating the Increase in Prices during a Bull Market? It Does Not Necessarily Mean That You Are a Skilled Trader

#11 The Newbie versus the Experienced Trader: The Main Differences

#9 What's the Worst Possible Start for You as a Trader? To Make a Profit on Your Very First Trade

When I placed my first trade on the stock market, I wished for a positive start. I wanted so much to close my first trade with a profit, which I did.

I thought it was the best start I could wish for. Looking back now, I realize it actually was the worst possible start for me as a trader. Because this (very lucky) event validated the assumption that made me decide to join the stock market roller coaster in the first place—I was convinced that making money on the market is easy; I was convinced that I too can be a successful trader.

During my first months, I also had loss-making trades. But somehow, in a strange way, the first profitable trade changed how I assessed my trading decisions and results. I focused on the wins, and I ignored the losses. When my forecasts proved to be correct and I won, it meant that I was a good trader. When the market moved against me and I lost, it was not my fault—the market moved in the "wrong" direction.

If my first trade had been a loss-making one, it would have changed my perception about trading. I would have realized from the beginning that losing is possible and even more likely than winning.

#10 Do You Succeed in Making Money by Speculating the Increase in Prices during a Bull Market? It Does Not Necessarily Mean That You Are a Skilled Trader

When 90 percent of the traded stocks go up because the market is in a bull cycle, if you are not profitable, it means that you are pretty unlucky. If you do manage to generate profits, there are two possible explanations for it: either you are a skilled trader who knows what he's doing, or you are the right person in the right place at the right time.

If you are just the right person in the right place at the right time, it's not necessarily a bad thing. However, it's important for you to understand and realize that you are profitable not because you have super strong trading skills but because you find yourself in a favorable context, and you do have a little bit of luck (at least).

If you are the right person in the right place at the right time, but you are not aware of this, and you start to see yourself as a professional and successful trader...well, the market will (brutally) bring you back to reality sooner or later.

#11 The Newbie versus the Experienced Trader: The Main Differences

The experienced trader has solid knowledge about fundamental and technical analysis, risk management, and investment psychology. Over time, he has developed, tested, and improved his trading strategy and his risk management strategy. He is disciplined, and he respects his rules.

The experienced trader understands that during a bull market there are also pullbacks—moments when the prices go down followed by a resumption of the uptrend. When he anticipates a deeper market correction, he decreases his market exposure. This means that he sells a part (or all) of the securities held in his portfolio and buys the securities later at lower prices. And most of the time, the experienced trader accurately foresees such corrections of the overall uptrend.

The experienced trader knows when something smells fishy, when a deeper market pullback actually turns into a bear market. When he liquidates his portfolio, he may not sell on the top. He might not sell short the bear cycle, but at least he protects most of the profits he made during the previous bull market. And when the prices reach the bottom, he is there, planning his strategy for the new uptrend.

Unlike the experienced trader, the newbie does not know much. He has neither a clear strategy nor a risk management system. He trades following his intuition. Because he has no clear rules, he trades excessively. He buys a stock today and sells it after three days for a tiny profit, just enough to cover the commission he pays to his broker. He quickly opens another trade as he identifies a new trading opportunity. After five more days, he realizes that his bet failed. He decides to close his position, this time with a loss. He buys again the first stock that meanwhile went up 10 percent, and he sells it few days later for a small profit. Overall he does a great job earning nice commissions for his broker. And if he is lucky enough, he does not lose his initial money.

In the end, the main difference is this: for a specific time frame, the experienced trader usually obtains higher returns compared to the average market return; the lucky newbie can get some profits, but usually his returns are significantly lower compared to the average market return.

Part 5: Trading on Demo Accounts

#12 If You Understand How It Works, It Doesn't Mean You Know How to Use It

#13 Don't Use Your Demo Account to Play for Fun. Take Your Practice Period Seriously

Let's See How Being a Trader Might Look and Feel Like

Let's Draw Some Conclusions

#14 The Invisible Trap of Trading on Demo Accounts

#12 If You Understand How It Works, It Doesn't Mean You Know How to Use It

Since one of your friends bragged with the profits he had made on the stock market, you became interested in trading. Because you are the kind of person who prefers to understand what something is about, before taking any decisions and actions, you started to study about investments and trading. During the past six months you covered the most important aspects. You learned about the history of the stock markets, the current mechanisms of the exchanges, and the ABC of trading—fundamental analysis, technical analysis, and risk management. You even read case studies and materials about the major financial crises and market crashes.

You now feel prepared. You believe that you have the necessary know-how to open a trading account and start trading the markets, risking your hard-earned money.

Don't take any hasty decisions! If you understand how something works, it does not necessarily mean that you know how to properly use it. For example, you may understand the theory of business management (maybe you studied at university), but it doesn't mean that starting tomorrow you can be the general manager of a company with twenty employees.

Having solid theoretical knowledge about trading is necessary (but not enough). It doesn't mean you are ready to risk on the market 100 percent, 50 percent, or even 10 percent of your hard-earned money. Remember: trading the markets is a battle between you and the other participants—individual traders and investors, investment funds, banks, etc., and one of the rules is "Eat or be eaten." So what should you do next?

Open a free demo trading account with a broker and practice. A demo account is an account with virtual money. You gain access to an online trading platform that allows you to see the prices of different financial instruments and buy and sell them. The demo account gives you the chance to test trading without any risks, because you do not trade with your own money. You trade with virtual money, meaning that the profits and losses you generate are also virtual. Trading on a demo account has no impact on your real financial situation.

#13 Don't Use Your Demo Account to Play for Fun. Take Your Practice Period Seriously

You decide to open a demo account. Please take a moment to understand your goals. Why are you doing this? Because you want to: prepare yourself for the real thing; test trading in a risk-free environment; apply your theoretical knowledge; make mistakes, learn from them, and start all over again; build your trading strategy and your risk management system to test and improve them; and see how trading works and understand whether or not trading is suitable for you. In order to achieve these goals, you need to take your trading practice seriously.

Some traders make the following mistake: because they are aware they cannot win or lose real money, they end up trading on the demo account for fun. Instead of practicing, they are just playing. Let's see some examples:

+ They trade randomly, buying and selling without any proper analyses to support their trading decisions.

+ They don't set trading rules.

+ If they do set some trading rules, they don't respect them.

+ They don't develop a trading strategy.

+ They don't improve their trading skills.

+ They don't learn much; they just have fun.

This approach can be quite costly. After playing for a while on a demo account, they might decide to open a real account and start trading with their money. Now tell me, do they stand a chance to be profitable?

If you want to avoid this trap, you need to take your demo trading practice seriously. Think and act as if the account is a real one with your money. Simulate the real thing as much as possible, and always keep your goal in mind: you want to learn, not to play and have fun.

(By the way if you plan to trade with X dollars, then ask your broker to adjust the balance of the demo account to X dollars so that you can practice and trade in similar conditions as you would on a real account.)

Let's See How Being a Trader Might Look and Feel Like

You choose your broker and open a demo account. A few days later, you receive a call from one of the broker's representatives. He presents you some details about his company and the services they offer, and you explain him that your goal is to practice trading on the demo account to see how it works. The guy asks if you prefer to have a specific balance on your demo account. Although you don't plan to trade with real money anytime soon, when that moment will come, you intend to start trading with $10,000. So you ask the guy to set the demo account's balance at $10,000.

While waiting for his confirmation, an idea pops into your mind: you will never have the chance to trade with a large amount of money—$10 million, for example—and you are really curious to see how it might feel like to trade the markets like a big player. After few more minutes, your demo account balance is set at $100 million in virtual money; you have decided to play the role of a hedge fund manager. It should be fun!

Strike one: Your goal was to test trading on a demo account and to practice, learn, and simulate a real account trading experience. Instead, you chose to play.

You are logged into the demo account. You see the balance: $100 million. You feel powerful. It's time to start trading. You check the quotes; you open and analyze the charts.

At one point, you identify a possible trade opportunity: on the four-hours chart, the price of XYZ just broke a resistance level after moving sideways over the last five days. You believe the price might go up, and you want to buy. According to your own set of rules, in case of a speculation, you can trade with maximum 10 percent of your total account value. This means $10 million. Hmm...but what should you do with the rest—$90 million? You have so much money; you can play big! So you decide to buy XYZ for $40 million.

Your decision to go long proves to be correct, and during the next hour, the price is up 2 percent: you have a profit of $800,000. Nice, even if it's virtual money! You consider that the price still has upside potential, and you decide to put the rest of the money to work for you: with the $60 million available in your demo account, you buy more XYZ. You didn't forget your "never go in with all your money" rule, but hey...you're trading on a demo account; you cannot lose real money! You just want to have some fun.

By the end of the trading session, you close your speculation, taking a total profit of $2,450,000 in virtual money. The price increased more than you expected. It really was a good day. You really had fun!

Strike two: Instead of testing your ideas, your theoretical knowledge, your trading strategies—to see what works and what doesn't, understand what you need to optimize and how you can do this—you chose to continue playing, ignoring all your rules.

During the next few weeks, you continue to "practice" trading on your demo account. You buy and sell like a crazy person, without any proper analyses to support your trading decisions: few quick looks on a chart, and you act mainly on your gut instincts. In one trade you win $3 million; in another one you lose $2 million, and so on. You really enjoy this. There is no big difference between you and a compulsive gambler who places bet after bet, hoping to hit the jackpot.

Three weeks after you have started "practicing" on your demo account, you have a profit of $7 million in virtual money, meaning 7 percent return in just three weeks! You are happy and proud with your result. Trading is easy. You feel confident and prepared to make your next step: trading with your hard-earned money.

Strike three: You don't understand that your practice period was actually a complete failure. For three weeks, you played with large amount of (virtual) money instead of practicing with an amount similar to the one you would actually want to invest. You ignored your trading rules, and you ended up trading like a gambler. You are convinced that trading is easy and that you are pretty good at it. You confuse knowledge and skills with pure luck. And now you are about to make a terrible mistake: you feel ready to trade with your own money on a real account.

You're in for a big surprise!

Let's Draw Some Conclusions

Be aware of your goal. Why did you create a demo trading account? You created it to test trading and to learn. This is why you need to take your practice period seriously.

Make proper analyses; support your trading decisions with arguments. Develop and test your rules and strategies, optimize them, and test them again. Analyze your past trades, learn from your mistakes, and understand what you can do differently (better) in the future. And remember: simulate as much as possible the real thing.

Practice trading on the demo account as much as you need; there is no general rule here. For one person six months can be enough. Another one might need one year and a half. Take your time. Don't hurry.

Last but not least: during your practice period, you might reach the conclusion that trading is not suitable for you. Maybe you find it too risky, and you are not actually comfortable losing your hard-earned dollars. Or maybe you find it too difficult, because even though you have learned a lot, you still do not understand what makes prices go up or down. Or you may feel so because of some other reasons.

If you realize that you don't have what it takes to trade the markets, that's actually great. Don't trade. Trading the markets is *not* suitable for everyone.

#14 The Invisible Trap of Trading on Demo Accounts

There are traders who treat seriously their practice period on demo trading accounts. They manage to gain experience, improve their skills, and build and optimize their trading systems and strategies. After a while, they even manage to consistently generate profits.

When they feel ready and prepared, they take the next step: they open a real trading account, and they start trading with their money. They apply the same principles, techniques, and strategies that worked while trading on the demo account. But somehow on the real account they don't get similar results. They even lose.

What's happening?

Trading on a demo account hides an invisible trap for the most of us: the lack of (intense) emotions. When you trade with your real money, the emotions are so much more intense than when you trade on a demo account.

Even if you do your best to simulate the demo practice as the real thing, on a deeper level you know that there is no real stake. This keeps you more calm and rational: it's easier to stick to your rules; it's easier to assess possible trade opportunities, to decide when to open a trade, and when to take your profit or your loss. It's easier to make better decisions.

On a real account, you can either multiply or lose your money—*your money*, your hard-earned money! That's why the eternal enemies of any trader show up: Greed and Fear prowl around, trying to take control of your decisions, and sometimes they succeed: gripped by greed or fear, you will no longer respect your rules; you will take bad decisions, and you will lose.

Sometimes the loss will be small, and it will not affect you, but there will be times when the loss will be bigger than you can take.

Are there any solutions?

Part 6: Increase Your Peace of Mind & Win the War against Fear and Greed

#15 Don't Invest Money You Can't Afford to Lose

Let's See How Being a Trader Might Look and Feel Like

#16 If You Decide to Start Trading on a Real Account, Don't Invest from the Very Beginning the Entire Amount You Are Willing to Allocate for Trading

#17 When You Trade the Markets, It's Important to Really Understand How Much Risk You Are Willing to Take

Let's Draw Some Conclusions

#18 Take One Step Further, and Gain the Zen Attitude That Can Help You Improve Your Trading

#15 Don't Invest Money You Can't Afford to Lose

If you consider borrowing money in order to start trading, my advice is: "Don't Do it." Don't borrow money even from friends or family. If you lose your money, that's one thing. If you lose money you don't actually have, well, that's a completely different story.

If you have been saving money with a specific purpose in mind (for example, to make a down payment for a house, to buy a car, to pay for your children's tuition, etc.), and you want to start trading, before doing anything rash, ask yourself: "What will happen if I lose 10 percent from the money I plan to invest? How about 15 percent or even 30 percent?"

If your financial stability was to be affected, or if you found it difficult to overcome such a moment, then you should not trade. Let me put it this way: When you think about these possible negative scenarios, are you gripped by feelings of panic and anxiety? If that's the case, then trading might not be suitable for you, at least not in this particular moment of your life.

Trading with money you can afford to lose decreases the psychological pressure that you face during the moments when the market moves against you. This way, you have better chances to keep your calm and act rationally.

Let's See How Being a Trader Might Look and Feel Like

Let's assume that you have been saving money to make a down payment for a house. In this moment, you have around $120,000. You plan to make the purchase within the next year and a half.

In the past few months, your gym buddy (let's call him Dan) bragged several times about the profits he made on the stock market, being an active trader, buying low and selling high. That made you think: "Should I start trading instead of getting a pretty low interest rate for my bank deposits? Should I make my money work for me?" Your friend told you that a 10–20 percent return in a year is quite doable. You do a quick math: if you invest $60,000 for one year, and you get that nice 10 percent return, you will have a profit of $6,000. That's your net salary for one month. Nice!

You make your research, you choose your broker, you open a trading account, and full of hope you deposit $60,000. Now it's time to make your first trade. Your gym buddy mentioned something about a stock—XYZ. The price increased 50 percent during the last year and 15 percent during the last month. You read a lot of good things about the company in the financial news; you checked several online investment communities, and it seems that many investors love XYZ, saying that the uptrend will continue. You are convinced that XYZ is a solid trading opportunity, and you decide to go in with all your money. During the next two weeks, the price goes up 3 percent. You already have a profit of $1,800! Wow, it's easier than you thought.

During the next week, the price moves sideways, without a clear direction. According to Dan, it's gaining momentum for the next upward movement. During the next two weeks, the stock loses about 2.5 percent. You still have a (very) small profit, and Dan tells you that he is taking advantage of the drop to buy more; you check again the online investment communities, and the general feeling regarding XYZ is still positive. You have no reasons to worry.

During the next three weeks, the price continues (slowly but surely) to decline. You now have a loss of about 5 percent on your position, which means you are down $3,000 (compared to your initial investment). You feel stressed and anxious, although Dan keeps on telling you that everything will be OK.

During one particular trading session, XYZ tumbles another 3.5 percent. Your loss is now more than 8 percent. You check your portfolio: your stock value is $55,005, and the "Profit/Loss" column displays -$4,995. You realize that you lost about 4 percent from your total savings. You realize that $4,995 is your net salary for more than three weeks or what you can save during a period of three to four months.

All these thoughts make you go crazy. Your heart starts racing; your head starts spinning. You are gripped by a strong feeling of fear. What if the price continues to go down another 5–10 percent? Your loss will be huge! You can't afford to lose any more money; you need it for the down payment. Right now, your fear turns into panic. You can't take it anymore, so you decide to sell everything.

Trading is risky. You shouldn't have traded in the first place. What were you thinking?

You decide to forget about this unhappy event, the stock market, and Dan and carry on with your life. Four months later you run into Dan, who tells you that XYZ gained more than 40 percent since you sold, and he made a small fortune out of it.

You can't believe it. It's not possible. It makes no sense!

Well, actually it does.

First, you started trading without having the proper knowledge, without a trading strategy and a plan.

Second, you decided to buy XYZ based on someone else's opinion.

Third, when you bought the stock, the price was 50 percent up for the last twelve months and 15 percent up for the last month. You bought on a local high, right before a deep pullback. Because you gambled with money you could not afford to lose, you let fear take over. Your decision to sell was not rational—based on fundamental or technical aspects. It was an irrational one: the pressure was high, and you lost control because you were afraid, afraid of losing money you could not afford to lose.

#16 If You Decide to Start Trading on a Real Account, Don't Invest from the Very Beginning the Entire Amount You Are Willing to Allocate for Trading

You accumulated theoretical knowledge, and you practiced on a demo account; you created trading rules and strategies, and you tested and optimized them. You are comfortable with the risks associated with trading, and you now feel prepared to make your next move: to open a real account and start trading with your money.

You analyzed your financial situation, and you decided to allocate X dollars for trading the markets. If you are like many other traders, you will transfer the entire amount in your account, and you will start trading. You will try to apply everything that you learned and practiced while trading on the demo account.

But when emotions kick in, you will realize that trading with your real money is pretty different than trading with virtual money. The higher the stake of a trade, the more intense the emotions will become. You will make mistakes, and you will lose money.

A better approach might be to transfer, in the beginning, only a small part of the overall amount you are willing to risk on the market—let's say 10 percent. If you trade with a much smaller amount of money than initially planned, you have better chances to stay calm, control your emotions, and stick to your trading rules. Why?

Because there is a correlation between the stakes of the game and the intensity of the emotions you experience. When you trade with $10,000 of virtual money, there is no risk for you, and therefore it's easy to manage and control your emotions. Trading with $10,000 of your money—well, that's another story. For sure, emotions will kick in, pushing you to make bad decisions. But if you trade with only 10 percent (meaning $1,000 of your money), the emotions you will experience should feel less intense.

The bottom line: start small. Transfer 10 percent from the money you initially wanted to invest. Trade and see if you are comfortable with the risks. Trade and see if you can control your emotions. Only when you feel prepared to trade with a higher amount, take a second small step: transfer another 10 percent. And repeat the process.

#17 When You Trade the Markets, It's Important to Really Understand How Much Risk You Are Willing to Take

You believe you are comfortable trading the markets with $20,000. You want to start small, and you decide to transfer into your trading account only $2,000.

After two weeks, you are down $300. Although the value of the loss is not that big, you are upset, and you can't stop thinking about it. You understand that it's not a huge amount, and it's not like your financial stability was affected. You dig deeper to see what exactly bothers you. You are indeed disappointed that you made some bad trades, but it's more than just that. You are actually upset because you lost those $300.

You thought that you had the proper mind-set to manage a trading account with $20,000 and that you would easily accept the risk of losing a part of that amount. But now, you've lost only $300, and you're finding it difficult to get over it.

There are moments in life when we discover that there is a significant difference between how we see ourselves and how we actually are. For example, I may consider myself calm and rational, and yet there are (many) moments when I (easily) lose my temper. Or in your case, you think you can handle the pressure of trading with $20,000, and it turns out that you can't even get over losing $300.

When you trade the markets, it's important to really understand how much risk you are willing to take. So if you do realize that your aversion to risk is higher than you thought, don't fight it. Accept it, and reassess what "risk" really means to you.

In the end, you might decide to invest smaller amounts or even decide not to trade at all, which is great because one of the main abilities of a good trader is staying calm when the pressure is high. And you can't do that when you take more risk than you can actually handle.

Let's Draw Some Conclusions

Find out what is your risk tolerance.

You might think that you are prepared to manage a trading account funded with $5,000, $50,000, or even $500,000. Start small. Deposit only a small part of that amount (let's say 10 percent). Trade, observe, and monitor your reactions:

+ When you place a trade, are you calm or anxious?

+ If the price moves in your favor, and you start to have a profit on your trade, how do you feel?

+ If the price goes against you, and you start to lose money on your trade, do you feel fear? Or do you manage to stay calm?

+ What triggers you to take a profit or activate a stop-loss order, your trading rules or your emotions?

+ When you face a bigger loss, what feelings do you experience?

Looking for answers to these kinds of questions can help you assess whether you need to increase/decrease the amount from your trading account.

If you decide that you are prepared and comfortable to manage a bigger amount of money, don't forget to take a second small step: transfer another 10 percent.

#18 Take One Step Further, and Gain the Zen Attitude That Can Help You Improve Your Trading

For a long time, I made the same mistake as a lot of other traders: I saw and analyzed everything in terms of money. Here are few examples:

+ I have $10,000 in my trading account.

+ XYZ is quoted at $10.

+ On my long position on XYZ, I already have a profit of $400.

+ On my short position on XYZ, I have a loss of $300. If the price moves down 4 percent, I will lose another $250.

This kind of thinking affected my decision-making process. Seeing everything in terms of money—how much money I either won or lost on an open position, how much money I could win or lose in a particular trade, etc.—made me more vulnerable in front of greed and fear. It was harder to stick to my plan and rules when either fear or greed was pushing me to act foolishly.

When I realized how this factor influenced the profitability of my trades, I decided to stop analyzing things in terms of money. I found a substitute: units. I also stopped using and thinking in terms of profit or loss. I started to use the term "result" which could be either positive (+X units) or negative (–X units). Here are few examples:

+ I have 10,000 units in my trading account.

+ XYZ is quoted at 10 units.

+ On my long position on XYZ, I already have a profit of 400 units.

+ On my short position on XYZ, I have a loss of 300 units. If the price moves down 4 percent, I will lose another 250 units.

Since I got used to my new system that eliminated the notions of money, profit, and loss, I have become a more calm and rational trader.

Part 7: Your Emotional State Can Influence How You Interpret What Happens on the Market

#19 Negative Feelings and a Pessimistic Attitude Can Impact Your Trading Decisions

#20 The Personal Financial Crisis and the Trap of Desperately Looking to Generate Profits Today, Right Now!

#21 When Things Are Great in Your Life, and You See Everything through Rose-Colored Glasses, Stay Alert: You May Not Properly Distinguish the Market's Colors

#19 Negative Feelings and a Pessimistic Attitude Can Impact Your Trading Decisions

You're going through a rough patch. Perhaps things in your professional career are not as you hoped. Or you struggle to prevent your business from failing. Or maybe the relationship with your significant other doesn't work.

Regardless of the reason that makes you feel blue, you need to understand that your emotional state can influence how you interpret the market news and evolution. You might have the tendency to focus on the negative news, while ignoring or discounting the positive ones. And this can influence your trading decisions.

Let's say that during the last couple of months, the relationship between you and your boss got tense. That's why you experience an avalanche of feelings: you are frustrated and sad, you feel misunderstood and unappreciated, and you are even concerned that you might lose your job. Your self-esteem and morale are quite low.

One day, after an argument with your boss, you decide to take a small break and try to calm down. You make yourself a coffee, and then you log in to your trading platform to see what's new. You are particularly interested in XYZ's evolution.

Since you bought XYZ two months ago, the price moved sideways in a very tight range. During the past two weeks, you started to think about selling it. You know that usually after a sideways trend, the price can sharply move either up or down. You have currently a very small loss on the trade, and you are concerned that the loss might significantly increase if the price breaks the range to the downside.

You check the price: XYZ is down 0.4 percent. The entire market is in red territory, with the main indices losing between 0.5 and 1.5 percent. You sigh. Maybe you should sell while your loss is still small. What if the market sentiment continues to deteriorate? Maybe XYZ will break the range with a gap down, and you will be forced to take a big loss.

You have a negative feeling about it, and you decide to sell everything.

Five weeks later, XYZ is up more than 25 percent. You lost a pretty nice opportunity.

#20 The Personal Financial Crisis and the Trap of Desperately Looking to Generate Profits Today, Right Now!

We previously discussed how your emotional state can impact not only how you analyze the markets but also the result of your trades. A particular case is when you face a personal financial crisis. Maybe your employer just announced that salaries would be slashed by 30 percent, you just lost your job, or maybe your start-up failed. The causes of your financial problems can be diverse.

In such moments, you focus on identifying solutions to overcome the obstacles. If you are a trader, you may consider becoming more active on the market to identify more opportunities, trade more, and generate more profit as soon as possible.

You are about to fall into a trap. When you *must* win money fast, when you feel the pressure to find trading opportunities *right now*, the chances to take bad trading decisions are quite high. Because when the stakes are high, it's more difficult to stay calm and analyze a possible trade in a rational and objective manner. If you chase fast profits, it's likely that you will desperately grab any trade that may seem like an opportunity. Most probably, you will end up overtrading and losing money.

Also please allow me to remind you an idea we discussed in a previous chapter: "don't trade with money you can't afford to lose." If you face a personal financial crisis, it means that the loss of a single dollar from your trading account will actually make things worse. If you try to put an end to your financial problems by making some "smart trades" on the market, you are actually one step away from taking irrational decisions affected by your emotions. Unless you are extremely lucky, your "smart trades" will turn into rash decisions. Most probably, you will end up losing money, and your financial problems will get worse.

#21 When Things Are Great in Your Life, and You See Everything through Rose-Colored Glasses, Stay Alert: You May Not Properly Distinguish the Market's Colors

When you succeed in anything that you do, when you feel confident that nothing can go wrong, when you start to believe that any action or decision that you take is the right one, when your level of optimism is at its peak, it's important to remain alert and cautious when you log in to your trading account.

Such moments can be dangerous. First, your high level of optimism can affect how you interpret the market news and evolution: you may have the tendency to focus on the positive news while ignoring or discounting the negative ones. Second, if you feel invincible and indestructible, if you are overconfident, then you may find yourself willing to take more risk and neglect your trading rules.

Sooner or later, this state of overconfidence will "help" you make few bad trades and lose money. How to avoid this? When you see life through rose-colored glasses, be aware of this and take them off before you log in to your trading account.

Part 8: On Profits and Losses

#22 You Just Made a Nice Profit on Your Trade. Take a Step Back, and "Press the Reset Button." Don't Enter Immediately into the Market, Chasing New Opportunities

#23 Did You Just Lose a Significant Amount of Money? Resist the Urge to Get Back into the Market and Recover Your Losses

#24 Losing an Opportunity Is Not the Same Thing as Losing Your Own Money

#22 You Just Made a Nice Profit on Your Trade. Take a Step Back, and "Press the Reset Button." Don't Enter Immediately into the Market, Chasing New Opportunities

One of your trades turned out to be very profitable for you: in less than two weeks, you won around $6,500. That's your net salary for one month and a half! Good job! You feel great about yourself. You feel powerful, confident, strong, invincible, like nothing can stop you, not even the market. You feel like you have this superpower to accurately predict how the market is going to move and that you can't fail!

Let me stop you right here and bring you back down to earth. You are not actually invincible. You just feel like this because you obtained a big profit, and it made you euphoric and overconfident. The bigger the profit is, the stronger the feeling of overconfidence grows. If you are like many other traders, you may feel the urge to get back into the market, looking for new trading opportunities, right now. Because you had a good run, you feel that you are in the zone, and you want to maximize this moment as much as possible. Unfortunately you face a great danger, and you don't even know it.

Don't get me wrong: it's OK to be confident and to trust your decisions and act accordingly. But being overconfident, well, that's a completely different story. When you are overconfident, you have no doubts regarding your decisions, regarding the arguments that support your decisions. You are 200 percent certain that the market will move as you predict. You are willing to take more risks and "temporarily" adjust your trading rules so that you can take full advantage of this moment while you are in the zone.

The market has its own way to "cure" a trader who "suffers" from overconfidence.

The overconfidence in your ability to forecast the market's direction
+ the urge to maximize your good run
+ increased willingness to take more risks and to neglect your trading rules
+ increased probability to discount risks
= high probability to make bad trades and lose (a lot of) money.

But this doesn't have to be your story. You can bring yourself back down to earth, without falling from the market roller coaster and losing any money.

When you make a nice profit on a trade, resist the temptation to immediately get back into the game. Take a step back. Reset yourself.

#23 Did You Just Lose a Significant Amount of Money? Resist the Urge to Get Back into the Market and Recover Your Losses

Losing money—it's no fun. Some traders quantify their loss saying: "I lost my salary for two months!" or "I can't believe that I blew 5 percent of my savings." Some take it personally saying: "I am a complete failure." Others are concerned with what their family and friends may think about them.

The solution that can make all their problems go away is obvious: they have to get back into the game and win money fast. The urge to recover their losses is irresistible. The bigger the loss is, the stronger the temptation to trade becomes.

This kind of moments can be very dangerous. As long as they are still affected by the recent loss, it's likely that they can't think clear and rational. In their chase for fast profits, they are willing to take more risks and neglect their trading rules.

Unfortunately the traders who fall into the trap, they usually end up making more bad trades and losing more money.

Imagine that you just closed a trade, and you took a loss of $2,000. You can't stop thinking that you lost your salary for two weeks. And it's not just this one bad trade. You had a bad month and a lousy quarter.

You are sad, angry, frustrated. You feel like a total loser. Your morale is low; your self-esteem is even lower. You just hope that during the next weeks, none of your friends will joke around, asking if you won your first million bucks in the market. You desperately search for any solution. There may be a quick fix: you just need a little bit of luck to win a fast $3,000–4,000. You made profits before; you can do it again.

Unfortunately you don't realize that you are not able to think rationally. Your emotional stability is still affected by your losses. You are no longer a trader. You are a gambler, willing to place bet after bet, hoping that your luck will turn around.

Two weeks later, you overtraded and placed more than thirty trades. You lost another $1,500. You decide it's time to stop, take a break, reboot, and regain your emotional strength. You should have done this in the first place.

#24 Losing an Opportunity Is Not the Same Thing as Losing Your Own Money

Many traders make the following mistake: when they miss a trading opportunity, they feel as if they lost money from their trading account. It's a dangerous mix-up. As we discussed in the previous chapter, when facing a loss, we may feel the urge to gain something in return, and we can easily end up taking more risks, overtrading, and losing money.

Let's say that you recently identified a stock XYZ. During the past three months, the price gained more than 40 percent. After the strong uptrend, the price started to move sideways, in a tight range. You believe there is a high probability for the price to continue its upward movement. However, you don't want to buy while XYZ remains inside the consolidation pattern. You prefer to go the safe way and wait for a strong "buy" signal: when the price will break through the resistance level of the range. You decide to closely monitor XYZ.

During one trading session, the bulls manage to push the price higher, breaking through the resistance level. This is the signal you have expected to see. But currently you have some doubts: XYZ is up 7 percent on a light trading volume, and you are afraid not to fall into a bull trap (meaning that it's a false breakout). So you decide to wait.

Within the next thirty minutes, the buyers push the price even higher. You realize that it's not a false breakout, but you are still reluctant to buy. XYZ is now 10 percent up, and you think that the price may suffer a pullback. Unfortunately the price continues to surge, and by the end of the trading session, XYZ is up +13 percent. The next day, XYZ opens with an upside gap: +7 percent. You regret you didn't buy yesterday, but now it's too late. The price gained 20 percent in less than two days. That's it, you lost the opportunity.

Your plan was to invest around $10,000. You are angry and frustrated. You identified the stock, and you watched it closely for several weeks. If you had bought, you would have made a profit of $2,000 in just two days. It's incredible. How could you lose $2,000?

This is a crucial moment: "If I had bought, I would have made a profit of $2,000" becomes "I just lost $2,000."

You missed an opportunity. It's important to understand that you didn't actually lose money from your trading account.

There will be other opportunities. Keep your eyes on the ball, and keep your calm so that you can take rational decisions.

Part 9: Two Things You Should Not Neglect

#25 Don't Ignore the Importance of Investment Psychology

#26 Keep a Trading Journal, Make a Habit of Writing Everything Down, and Don't Stop

#25 Don't Ignore the Importance of Investment Psychology

There are traders who have solid theoretical knowledge, ranging from fundamental analysis to technical analysis and risk management. They succeeded to build decent, and even good trading strategies and risk management systems. However, they are not profitable. They may consider that the problem is their trading system, which they think doesn't work properly and needs to be adjusted.

They don't realize that there may be another cause for their problem: investment psychology—how our human nature compels us to make bad investment decisions.

Let's take an example outside the area of trading. Imagine a professional tennis player. She has developed a very good physical condition and strong tennis techniques, tactics, and skills. She practices each day for six to eight hours to stay in shape and constantly improve her abilities. Let's assume that her main focus was, and still is, on the technical side, neglecting the psychological training. How do you think she will behave during a match if she makes two consecutive unforced errors or if, in the deciding set, she is led 5–4 at games, and her opponent serves for game, set, and match?

During high-pressure situations, the psychological factors play a crucial role: they can make the difference between success and failure; in the case of a trader, between profit and loss.

#26 Keep a Trading Journal, Make a Habit of Writing Everything Down, and Don't Stop

For a trader, it's very important to understand the "whys." Why did he decide to open a trade? Why did he choose that exact moment to open his position? How did he feel when he opened the trade? Was his decision a rational one, or maybe was it motivated by greed? Why did he close the position? What were the factors that contributed to his profit/loss? Did he predict all these factors? How did he feel when the price fluctuated, moving either against him or in his favor?

If you assess your past trading decisions, you can discover the patterns that you use to analyze and trade the markets. And that's why you should keep a trading journal: because you have better chances to improve your trading, by removing the bad habits and introducing new, better ones.

It sounds simple, right? Analyze the past, learn from it, and take better actions in the future. Well, it's a lot harder than it sounds. While everybody can keep a trading journal, only few can do it the proper way, and it's usually these guys who manage to boost their trading skills.

Here are some examples of obstacles you may encounter:

Instead of writing down the naked truth, you are tempted to find excuses.
Sometimes we can't handle the truth because it changes how we see ourselves, and it can hit our self-esteem. Sometimes it's more convenient to rationalize and find excuses. It may work in the short run as we manage to keep our self-esteem intact. In the long run, however, it's definitely not a healthy solution, because

we end up making the same mistakes, over and over again. Let's take an example.

You have a long position on XYZ. Unfortunately the price started to slide, and three days later you have a loss of $720. During the trading session, XYZ further declines. On the open positions' window you can see how your loss gets deeper and deeper: -$725, -$732, -$741. Your heart starts beating faster, and you can't breathe. You are gripped by fear, seeing -$745 and -$752. What should you do? Should you sell?

You don't have any logical reasons to believe that the arguments that made you buy in the first place are no longer valid. Moreover when you entered the trade, you decided to activate your stop loss at -$1,500. Basically there is no rational reason for you to sell, but the loss deepens, and you can't stand the thought of losing another dollar. The pressure is too high, and you decide to sell everything.

When you have to write down in your trading journal, it's hard for you to admit that you panicked. You see yourself as a calm, strong, and rational person, able to successfully manage difficult situations. The naked truth is hard to accept. So you choose the more convenient "solution." You rationalize: you decided to activate your stop-loss order sooner, because the downward movement was very aggressive, and it made you doubt that the price would recover.

Unfortunately the only one that gets tricked is you. You just missed the opportunity to become a better trader.

You don't take it seriously.

You constantly write down in your trading journal, but you don't make the necessary effort to really understand why you act the way you do. One day you are in a hurry, another day you are not in the mood. No matter the reason, you don't extract any useful insights from this activity

Eventually you stop making notes in your trading journal.

So if you decide to keep a trading journal...be honest. Do your best to really understand why you act the way you do. Identify your habits and patterns. Adjust your trading rules accordingly.

Don't stop.

Part 10: Don't Let Your Losses Kill Your Account

#27 Use Stop-Loss Orders. When the Market Moves against You, the Hope That the Price Will Recover Is Dangerous: It Can Actually Kill Your Account

#28 Don't Randomly Set Your Stop-Loss Order. Identify Key Price Levels

#29 The Trap of the Stop-Loss Order

Stop-Loss Hunting: How the Big Investors Try to Maximize Their Profits at Others' Expense

Let's Draw Some Conclusions

#27 Use Stop-Loss Orders. When the Market Moves against You, the Hope That the Price Will Recover Is Dangerous: It Can Actually Kill Your Account

When you enter a trade, you have positive expectations. You anticipate the price to work in your favor. If you are right, you will make a profit.

What happens if you are wrong, and the price moves against your position? Many traders hope that the price will recover. If they are lucky enough, it may happen like this. If not, they will end up with a pretty nice loss.

Before you open a new trade, you need to prepare for the negative scenario, in case your forecast turns out to be incorrect, and you start losing. Ask yourself how much money are you willing to lose on that trade? Accept the fact that the worst may happen, meaning that you can actually lose that amount. After that, use stop-loss orders to limit a possible loss.

Let's take a very simple and basic example to see how stop-loss orders work.

XYZ is traded at $10. A trader anticipates that the price may increase toward $13-14, and he decides to buy. He is aware that his forecast may not be correct. If the price starts to go down, he is not willing to accept a loss bigger than 10 percent of the invested amount. He sets a stop-loss order at $9. What does it mean? If the price slides 10 percent, to $9, his stop-loss order becomes active, and all his XYZ securities are sold at market price[i], limiting his loss in case the price continues to move down.

Using stop-loss orders is critical for the safety of your account. If you don't use stop-loss orders, it may happen that you lose a significant amount of money on a single poor trade. When trading the markets, learning to limit your losses is essential.

#28 Don't Randomly Set Your Stop-Loss Order. Identify Key Price Levels

You find out about stop-loss orders. It sounds good: it helps you limit your losses. Instead of losing $3, you only lose $1. That's great, right? So you start using stop-loss orders.

During a trading session, you decide to make a short-term speculation. You want to buy XYZ at $15, because you believe it may go toward $15.50, generating more than 3 percent return. You open the trade, and you remember that you should also set a stop-loss order to limit the loss in case your forecast proves to be incorrect. Where should you set it? You choose $14.90. (If somebody asks you why you chose this level, most probably you will reply, "Why not?").

You are all set now: even if the price drops, you have the stop-loss order to protect you. For the next few hours, you work on some of your other tasks. When you log in to your trading account three hours later, you see that XYZ is traded at $15.60. The price moved even faster and better than you expected, and you decide to close your trade, and take the profit. But...you don't understand what happened...because the position is already closed! How is this possible? You check your trading history: the price went down to $14.88, your stop-loss order became active, and your position was closed with a loss. Then, the price sharply recovered, and it went up, exactly how you anticipated. You are frustrated: instead of taking a profit, you took a loss!

This happens several times, so your draw a conclusion: stop-loss orders are not working for you. Please allow me to offer a different view. You usually set the stop-loss level randomly. Instead, you should identify a key price level, and set your stop-loss order in that area. A key price level represents a particular price level whose break gives a strong signal that your forecast may no longer be valid and that there is a high probability for the price to continue its move against your position.

Let's say that the difference between the current price and the key price level identified by you is four percentage points. You can set your stop-loss level a little bit wider, for example, six percentage points from the current price. (We will discuss later on the reasons for this.) Then, ask yourself how much money you can afford to lose in this trade. Let's assume you say $500. This means that you can invest a maximum amount of $8,333.

Let's recap: You want to buy XYZ with $8,333. According to your research, if the price moves down 4 percent, it breaks a key price level, and this is a strong signal that the downtrend may continue. You set your stop-loss order a little bit wider, for example, six percentage points below the current price. The loss should be limited around the value of $8,333 × 6% = $500[ii]. You are comfortable with this level, and you decide to enter the trade.

#29 The Trap of the Stop-Loss Order

Many individual traders can find themselves saying: "I always trade using stop-loss orders. There were moments when the stop-loss order helped me avoid a big loss. There were also plenty of trades when the price moved initially against me and activated my stop-loss order. Soon after that, the price started to recover and moved exactly as I anticipated. In such cases, not only did I take a small loss, but I also missed the opportunity to make a nice profit although my initial forecast proved to be correct."

The conclusion: "I find it very strange. It's like somebody knows where I placed my stop-loss order and intentionally pushes the price there to close my position."

What would you say if I told you that you are not far from being correct? There are market participants who try to anticipate the price levels where other traders might have placed their stop-loss orders. They even try to push the market price in that area, hoping to trigger the activation of the stop-loss orders. And sometimes they succeed. It's what they call stop-loss hunting.

Please, stay calm. It's not magic, it's not a conspiracy, and you should not take it personally. The explanation is quite simple: these market participants (usually big professional investors) try to maximize their profits. Sometimes they do it at other traders' expense. "Eat or be eaten," remember?

Before we take an example to see how stop-loss hunting works, it's important to understand that most of the traders use the same principles and techniques to establish the key price levels where they set the stop-loss orders. Of course, there is a certain degree of subjectivity involved in the process. However, there are cases when a significant number of market participants set the stop-loss orders in a similar (tight) area.

One more thing: the stop-loss hunting process has better chances to succeed if the player who is going in for the kill is financially strong. This way he has better chances to move the price and trigger the stop-loss orders.

Let's see how it works.

Stop-Loss Hunting: How the Big Investors Try to Maximize Their Profits at Others' Expense

Let's say that ABCDE is a big, high-risk investment fund trading on several financial markets around the globe.

Let's assume that two weeks ago ABCDE bought 1.2 million XYZ securities at prices between 80.00 - 85.00 units. The average price was 83.50 units per security. Since then, XYZ went up, and the price managed to break the psychological level of 100.00 units. The current market price is 101.00 units.

The traders who manage ABCDE estimate that XYZ may have a short-term pullback between 1 and 3 percent, because the price gained more than 20 percent in just two weeks, and for sure, some traders and investors will be tempted to take their profits off the table. ABCDE's internal research forecasts a possible price between 140 and 150 units within the next three to six months. That's why the traders from ABCDE want to increase the fund's exposure on XYZ to 2.5 million securities and maximize the profits as much as possible.

ABCDE's traders believe that there are a lot of stop-loss orders between 97 and 99 units. They reached this conclusion by using technical-analysis techniques, and by taking into account factors related to investment psychology.

Moreover they estimate that it will be necessary to sell around 600,000 XYZ in order to push the price down from 101 units to 99 units. Once the price hits 99 units, the stop-loss orders will get activated, meaning that the supply will increase, and the price will continue to slide below 99 units. This will trigger more stop-loss orders to get activated, and with a little bit of luck, the domino effect will push the price lower and lower, toward 97 units, and maybe even lower, to 95 or 93 units.

As the price slides, ABCDE will start buying back the 600,000 securities (sold between 101.00 and 99.00 units), and they will continue to buy until they reach their target exposure of 2.5 million XYZ securities.

At first, they will send into the market small-sized "buy" orders. As they get closer to their target exposure, they will send into the market bigger orders. This will act as a signal for the other participants, letting them know that an important investor is buying, and it will offer an impulse to other traders to buy as well.

Once the stop-loss orders are executed, the pressure on the "sell" side will decrease, while the "buy" orders will multiply. The demand for XYZ will become higher than the supply, and the price will start to move up.

In a favorable scenario for ABCDE's traders, the price will surpass again the level of 100 units. The abrupt pullback, followed by an even more abrupt rally, will encourage more and more traders to go long during the following trading sessions. And this might actually trigger the uptrend toward 140–150 units.

Only one thing will be missing: hitting the "Enter" key on the keyboard to sell the 600,000 securities in the market.

At the end of this process, ABCDE will sell 600,000 XYZs between 101 and 99 units. When the price goes down, they will manage to buy back the securities at prices between 97 and 99 units. ABCDE will buy another 1.3 million securities at prices between 93 and 97 units and successfully reach the target exposure of 2.5 million securities.

Three months later, ABCDE will sell everything at prices between 145 and 150 units.

Let's Draw Some Conclusions

For many traders, obtaining the profits is the main goal. After more than eleven years of trading, I believe that you should build your trading mind-set on two main pillars:

+ not losing your initial funds, and

+ obtaining a positive return.

Whenever you place a trade, you do it because you trust your forecast. It's important to be aware that there are (many) moments when your forecast proves to be incorrect, and you lose money. The question is: How much money are you going to lose?

When the price moves against you, hoping that it will recover is not the proper solution. You need to use stop-loss orders so that you have control over your possible losses.

Do not randomly set your stop-loss levels. Otherwise there will be (many) trades when the price will move against you, your stop loss will be hit, and your position will be closed with a loss; soon after that, the price will recover, and it will move as you initially anticipated. You will take a small loss, and you will miss an opportunity to make a nice profit. You will end up frustrated and distrustful in your abilities as a trader.

Identify the key price level whose break may invalidate your scenario. When you set the stop-loss level, don't forget about stop-loss hunting, and make sure to include a buffer zone.

Do a quick calculation: if your stop-loss order is activated, how much money are you going to lose on your trade? Are you comfortable with the value of the loss? If not, you need to decrease the value of your trade.

Last but not least, don't give up using stop-loss orders. Trading is a game of probabilities. If you use stop-loss orders, you may miss some opportunities (when the price recovers just after your stop-loss order was activated), but you will avoid those few moments when you could lose a fortune.

Part 11: Enhance Your Trading: Take-Profit Level and Risk-Reward Ratio

#30 Making a Profit on a Trade Requires Two Steps: Forecasting the Market Direction Correctly and Actually Taking the Profit Off the Table

#31 How Do You Decide If It's Convenient to Place a Trade? Calculate the Risk-Reward Ratio

#30 Making a Profit on a Trade Requires Two Steps: Forecasting the Market Direction Correctly and Actually Taking the Profit Off the Table

Many traders open a position without having a clear target price in mind. If they open a trade (i.e., if they either buy or sell), they do it because they expect the price to move (either up or down). As to how much it will move, ±5 percent, ±10 percent, ±20 percent, or maybe ±40 percent, they don't have a clear target. They are rather interested to see that their forecast—in terms of market direction (either up or down)—is correct. So they just enter the trade and hope for the best.

They lose sight of the fact that a profit is not generated just because the price goes as they predicted. It's actually necessary to lock in the profit by closing the winning position.

Let's say that you expect XYZ to go up, and you buy it at $10. You don't have any clear expectation regarding a possible price target. You just hope the upside will be significant—the bigger, the better, right?

During the next few weeks, the market proves that you were right, and the price rockets to $12. You have a profit of $2 per one XYZ, and you start feeling that 'sky's the limit'. Your approach was, and still is, to wait and to see what happens. During the next trading sessions, the price dips to $11.80, then to $11.70, and further to $11.50. You are not (too) worried. You understand that it can be just a temporary pullback, and you still have a profit of $1.50 per one XYZ. You decide to wait and see, hoping that the price will recover. Unfortunately the decline becomes more aggressive. During the next two trading sessions, the price slides below $11.00. You panic and sell everything at $10.90.

Your profit of $2.00 (for one XYZ) became $1.50, and it actually turned out to be $0.90 when you sold, because a profit is locked in only when you close the trade.

If you expect the price to go up, it's not enough just to buy. You need to assess the upside potential; to estimate a target price where you plan to close your trade. And then, you actually need to close the trade and lock in the profit.

The same goes if you expect the price to go down. It's not enough to sell short. You need to assess the downside potential; to estimate a target price where you plan to close your trade and actually close it.

As long as the price does not move in new highs/new lows territory, you can use the past history to try to predict where the price may go. This can help you set your take-profit order[iii]. Of course, you will not be 100 percent accurate—nobody is—but at least you will have a target price in mind.

#31 How Do You Decide If It's Convenient to Place a Trade? Calculate the Risk-Reward Ratio

Before placing any trade, it's necessary to assess if the trade is worth the risk. Think about it this way. I have a lottery ticket that costs $1. Would you buy it for $1 if I said that most probably you might win fifty cents? No, because the cost is bigger than the possible reward. What if I told you that it's possible to win $3? This time you may want to consider buying the ticket, because you may win $3 on a ticket that costs only $1. In order to decide what to do, you compare the cost with the possible reward.

In trading, it's similar. You need to assess what you may lose and what you may win so that you can decide if a trade is worth the risk or not.

Before placing a trade, you need to establish the stop-loss and the take-profit levels. The stop-loss level helps you estimate how much you can lose if the market moves against you. The take-profit level helps you estimate how much you can win if your forecast is correct. Please be aware that the take-profit level is a target estimation made by you; the market price may or may not reach your target.

The next step is to compare the risk-reward ratio. In theory, a good ratio is 1:3, meaning that for each dollar you risk losing, you may get a profit of three dollars. In practice, there are traders that accept a risk-reward ratio of 1:2 or even 1:1. Below this level, the trade is no longer worth it. For example, if the risk-reward ratio is 1:0.75, this means that you risk losing one dollar in order to get a potential profit of seventy-five cents. The risk is bigger than the possible reward.

Let's take an example.

XYZ is traded at $10. You forecast an increase in the price. Before buying, you want to assess the risk-reward ratio. You do your research, and you conclude that the upside potential is 15–20 percent, meaning the price may reach $11.50 to $12.00. You decide to set your take-profit order at $11.50. The potential reward is $1.50 per one XYZ.

In case your forecast is wrong and the price slides, you consider that $9.50 is a key level. If the price decisively breaks below $9.50, you think that XYZ will further decline. You decide to set the stop-loss order at $9.30. The risk is $0.70 per one XYZ.

The risk-reward ratio is 0.7:1.5 or 1:2.1. You find it decent, and you decide to place the trade.

(Please be aware that the risk-reward ratio is subjective, because it's based on your estimation for the potential profit.)

Part 12: Solving the Informational Puzzle

#32 Too Much Information Can Hurt Your Decision-Making Process

Let's See How Being a Trader Might Look and Feel Like

#33 Be Careful Who You Trust

#34 Ask Yourself: "What Expertise and Credibility Does This Trader Have?"

#35 What Do You Actually Know about the Person "Hiding" behind a Username?

#36 You Will Not Strike Gold Just Because You Read the Financial Media

#37 What's the Deal with Trading Signals and Trading Robots?

#32 Too Much Information Can Hurt Your Decision-Making Process

When you trade the markets, you need to understand the current context and estimate what may happen in the future. To do this, you need information, and there is plenty of it out there. It's never been easier to have access to the latest news and events, as they can be easily accessed now through: online financial portals (free or paid), economic calendars, news feeds integrated directly into your trading platform, online financial forums and communities, research materials prepared by your broker or some financial advisory firms, trading signals, and many other means. You are literally attacked by information.

While information is necessary, too much information can actually confuse a trader, even an experienced one.

Think about it this way: each piece of information that you have is a piece of the puzzle that you try to solve. Solving the puzzle means finding answers to questions such as the following: "What should I buy/sell? What may be the proper timing to open my trade? Where should I set the stop-loss and take-profit orders? When should I close my position?" Basically, solving the puzzle means taking the correct trading decisions.

With each new information that you get, the pile of pieces you can use grows bigger and bigger. So it becomes harder and harder to solve the puzzle, because you have too many pieces, and you can't put them together. You don't know how.

Facing a high flow of information is particularly difficult for beginners because they don't know how to manage it, how to look for and extract those elements that can actually affect the prices, and how to interpret the information and transform it into actionable insight. They take bad trading decisions, and they make unprofitable trades. When trying to understand what happened, they mistakenly reach the conclusion that they need to be better informed. So they look for more sources of information.

Don't get me wrong: being properly informed is essential for success in trading. However, you need to realize that, from the ocean of information that you can easily access, only a fraction of it really makes a difference in demand and supply, thus having an impact on the prices. The rest is background noise, and the problem is that it makes you (many times) incapable of hearing what really matters.

Successful traders understand this. They monitor the flood of information, and they extract only those factors that can make the difference. They managed to develop their ability to separate the relevant from the background noise.

Let's See How Being a Trader Might Look and Feel Like

Your day just started. You drink your coffee while reading the economic and financial news. To be sure you are not missing out on anything, you track four international online portals and three local ones. You are mainly interested in global macroeconomics and stock markets, but you also want to be updated with the recent developments in both the Forex and the bond markets.

Before finishing your coffee, you skim through more than thirty articles. Usually the opinions and views are diverse: some economic journalists and financial experts are more optimistic; others are rather pessimistic; there are few that say a lot without actually saying anything, reaching conclusions such as: "It will get better if it doesn't get worse." You feel a little bit confused.

You sigh and open the macroeconomic calendar that helps you monitor the release of the most important economic indicators. You have filtered the calendar so that it displays only the indicators that may have an impact on the instruments you trade. Today twelve indicators are scheduled for release; it's going to be an eventful day.

Soon after that, you log in to your trading account. You want to be quickly updated with the latest news, so you have switched on the news feed. Every few minutes, a pop-up lets you know there is new information, a new article, a new research material available for you. You track the news based on their importance. During one regular day you skim and scan through fifteen to twenty "high importance" news items and twenty to twenty-five "moderate importance" ones. Most of the time, you find it difficult to extract the essence and turn it into actionable insight.

You try to filter the flood of information and reach a conclusion on your own, but it's hard to solve the "puzzle" when you have so many pieces to put together. In the end, you feel puzzled.

#33 Be Careful Who You Trust

When dealing with too much of confusing information, a lot of traders desperately search for solutions to help them identify trading ideas and opportunities. Here are few examples:

+ taking advices from different traders or investors they know

+ joining online trading communities and forums

+ looking for comments and ideas of different financial experts and/or economics journalists

+ trading signals and trading robots.

Discovering different views, ideas, and arguments is not a bad thing. Sometimes you may even get the chance to look at something from a completely different perspective. The problem is when your trading decisions rely exclusively on other people's comments and ideas. You need to filter everything through your own thinking process. If you just want to have someone telling you what to do, trading is not for you.

#34 Ask Yourself: "What Expertise and Credibility Does This Trader Have?"

During my first years as a trader, I used to meet, from time to time, with few other guys who shared my passion for trading. We all were beginners, and those get-togethers helped us feel that we were not alone on the market roller coaster. We were discussing the recent news and market developments, we were sharing our successes and failures, and we were debating possible trading opportunities.

I remember one meeting when another guy joined us, being invited by one of the members of our small club. Let's call him Mr. X. Mr. X was older than us, and apparently he was a successful investor in the stock market. He had been trading for a while, and during the recent years, he had made a killing. I remember that I saw him like a trading guru. He was everything I hoped I would become.

The meeting was amazing. Mr. X proved to be not only a great investor but also a talented storyteller. He shared with us his story: how he had begun to invest, his good times, and his bad ones. He seemed really experienced and professional, a true stock market veteran.

By the end of our meeting, we were anxious to hear Mr. X's forecasts and trading ideas. He was kind enough to tell us few stocks he was watching closely. The cherry on the cake was when he mentioned to us a stock that had outperformed the market in the previous months and had made him a lot of money. He told us that we should buy it, because it would continue to bring solid returns. We were ecstatic.

Just before we left, I had the inspiration to ask him how exactly he managed to spot that particular stock. Mr. X's answer left me speechless: "Well, I was checking the tab with stock tickers, and I noticed one that I really liked. I didn't know anything about it, but I had a gut feeling that I should bet on that stock. And so I did!"

The bottom line: when somebody gives you trading advices or ideas, ask yourself, what expertise and credibility does this trader have?

#35 What Do You Actually Know about the Person "Hiding" behind a Username?

Online communities and forums are very appealing to many traders. Joining a forum allows you to virtually interact with other people interested in trading. You can monitor the discussions; you can see other's views on how the markets may move. You can ask questions about the instruments that you trade, and you can understand other traders' ideas and opinions.

If you decide to join an online community, it's important to realize that you need to filter the information you get through your own thinking process. You have to avoid the trap of taking decisions relying too much, or worse, exclusively, on the ideas, comments, suggestions, advices, or recommendations offered by one user or another, even if it seems that the community respects, trusts, and follows him or her.

You need to ask yourself what you really know about the real person who writes as XYZ123 or some other username. You don't know who he is, and what he is doing for a living. You don't know if he has solid knowledge about trading. You don't know for how long he has been trading. You don't know if he just plays with virtual money on a demo account or if he trades on a real account with $100,000, $30,000, or with the loose change from his left pocket. You don't know his trading history. You don't know if he is a profitable trader or a loser. You don't know how exactly he takes his trading decisions and what risk management rules he applies. You don't know a lot of things.

So before placing a trade just because username XYZ123 wrote some message, ask yourself, what do you actually know about XYZ123?

#36 You Will Not Strike Gold Just Because You Read the Financial Media

There are traders who closely monitor the financial media, carefully reading opinions, comments, and forecasts of different economics journalists and financial experts. Their goal is to find trading opportunities. If a popular financial expert says that XYZ should go up, they buy. If the main conclusion of an article is that XYZ should go down, they sell. You should not trade solely on this kind of information, at least if you are interested in not losing your money.

What you need to understand about the financial experts and the economics journalists is this: although they may have more knowledge and more resources than the average trader, they are not wizards; they don't have a magic globe that accurately predicts how tomorrow will look like, how the markets will move. If they had, they would be (very) rich, and they would quit their jobs as brokers, financial analysts, or journalists, right?

It's not as though *all* the professionals working in the financial industry (brokers, financial analysts, advisors, asset managers, economics journalists, etc.) constantly win money from trading the markets. When we speak about winners and losers, you can bet that they come from both sides: finance professionals and ordinary traders.

You would be amazed how many "experts" are in the same dense fog as you are. Sure they use the fancy words, and they always find explanations for what has already happened. But when it comes to predicting the future…well, that is another story.

You also need to understand that, in general, most news and materials present what has already happened. By the time you read it, it's likely that the news has become outdated in the markets. Being aware of what happened yesterday or two hours ago and understanding why it happened—these are important. But when you trade the markets, in order to make profits, you need to forecast now what will happen during the next few hours, days, or weeks.

The bottom line: select few professional and trustworthy financial media. Monitor them; look for news, ideas, perspectives, and arguments. Select only what you believe is worthy, and add the information to your puzzle. Filter everything through your own thinking process. Don't buy or sell just because some hotshot said so.

#37 What's the Deal with Trading Signals and Trading Robots?

First things first.

What is a trading signal?

A trading signal is a trading idea or suggestion to place a trade on a specific financial instrument. It gives you information about the market direction that you should choose (either buying or selling), the price level at which you should open the trade, and the stop-loss and take-profit levels you should set. It can also offer the main arguments behind the trading signal. However, the trading decision is up to you: you decide whether you should act or not, when and at what price to open the position, and where to place the stop-loss and take-profit orders.

The trading signals are created either by a human or by automated trading software, built to generate the signals based on specific factors. In general, the signals are triggered by the use of technical analysis factors and/or mathematical models. Some trading signals—especially the ones created by humans—can incorporate fundamental analysis factors also.

A trader can buy trading signals from different trading signals providers, usually by paying a monthly fee.

What is a trading robot?

A trading robot is a software machine built to generate trading signals and automatically execute those trades on your account, usually without needing any interference from you. In general, the signals are triggered by the use of technical analysis factors and/or mathematical models. Trading robots are available for purchase over the internet.

Now coming back to the interesting part: do trading signals and trading robots work?

#1 To a beginner, such tools can be very appealing: instead of working hard on his or her own, somebody else tells him/her what to do. So he or she sits back and watches how the profit grows, right?

Wrong! There is no "Holy Grail" of trading. If there was one, we would all be millionaires.

#2 Think about it this way: if you managed to develop a trading system that works, if you were able to generate profits on the long run, why would you be interested in selling your solution to others? You could use it on your own trading account, and get all the profits.

For a signal provider/trading-robot owner, it's simpler to make money from selling the product to other traders than it is to make profits by using the same product to trade the markets. When they sell the product, they have no risk of losing money. If they traded the markets (using their product), they could either win or lose.

So be cautious. Don't believe everything you hear.

#3 If you discover offers that guarantee that you will make tons of money, you should stay away from them. Don't forget: when you trade the markets, the only sure thing is that there are no guarantees.

#4 Be aware that there is a lot of rubbish out there. The risk does not come from losing the money that you pay to buy the trading signals or the trading robot. The real risk arises from losing your hard-earned money while trading based on all that rubbish.

#5 If you decide to test trading signals or trading robots, do your homework. Search the web for reviews and opinions from real users. Take all the necessary steps to ensure that the provider is trustworthy. Once you buy such a solution, don't use it directly on your real trading account! Test it on a demo account in order to assess the results. Test it for longer periods of time: you may find that something works well for few days, weeks, or even months, but in the long run it may turn out to be unprofitable.

#6 Even if you find a decent provider, you still don't have any guarantees for success. Let's say that your trading signals provider has a 60 percent success rate (which is very good, by the way!). This means that from one hundred suggested trades, sixty prove to be good, while forty are incorrect. What if you decide to follow only twenty-five of the good trades and thirty-five of the bad ones? Or what if you take very large exposures in some of the bad trades, and your losses are big?

In the end, it all comes down to your own risk management system and how you decide to use the signals.

#7 So what is the bottom line?

#7.1 Trading robots: The benefit is that it eliminates the emotions from the decision-making process. However, I am not a big fan of buying a trading robot: I don't like to let others decide when it comes down to managing my money.

A better approach may be to develop your own trading systems, strategies, and rules, and then code your software (or hire an engineer to do it). Test it, see how it works, and improve it. Repeat the steps of the abovementioned development process.

#7.2 Trading signals: Don't buy or sell just because the signals are telling you to do so. Check the signal, read the arguments behind it, make your own research, and reach your own trading decision.

At the end of the day, if you prefer to have somebody else managing your investments, then trading the markets may not be for you. You may actually want to look for a professional and trustworthy asset management company that will create your risk profile and invest your money accordingly.

Part 13: About Margin Trading and Short Selling: the Trio Hope-Ecstasy-Agony Is Only One Click Away

What Is Margin Trading?

#38 Do You Understand That Margin Trading Amplifies Both the Profit and the Loss?

#39 Avoid the Trap of Seeing the Glass Half Full

#40 Don't Use Margin Trading to Place High-Risk Bets. Don't Trade like a Maniac

#41 The Invisible Risk of Margin Trading

Let's Draw Some Conclusions

What Is Short Selling?

#42 "You Can Win When Prices Fall" versus "There Is a Higher Probability to Lose If Your Forecasts Are Incorrect"

What Is Margin Trading[iv]?

The margin represents the amount of money you need to have available on your trading account in order to place the trade and maintain your open position.

Let's say that you want to have an exposure of $5,000 on XYZ.

If you do *not* trade on margin, in order to place the trade you need to have in your account the entire amount of $5,000.

If you trade on margin, then you need to have in your trading account only a fraction of those $5,000. Depending on several factors (including the country where you are from, the broker you choose to trade with, the financial instrument, etc.), the margin (as a percentage) can have different values. For example, 50 percent, 20 percent, 10 percent, or 5 percent, and it can be even lower, such as 1 percent, 0.50 percent, or 0.10 percent.

> 50% margin means that in order to place your trade, you need to have available in your account $5,000 × 50% = $2,500.

> 10% margin means that in order to place your trade, you need to have available in your account $5,000 × 10% = $500.

> 1% margin means that in order to place your trade, you need to have available in your account $5,000 × 1% = $50.

> 0.10% margin means that in order to place your trade, you need to have available in your account $5,000 × 0.10% = $5.

As the margin (as a percentage) decreases, you need less money in your trading account to open a trade and keep the open position.

In this moment, you may think: "Are you telling me that a 10 percent margin allows me to open a trade for $100,000, having in my account only $10,000? And that if the margin is 0.10 percent, I can trade $100,000 with as little as $100? Wow, this is awesome! I can make tons of money now! Everybody should trade on margin! How can I start?"

If that's the case, please calm down. Now, tell me: do you still believe in Santa Claus? I hope not.

#38 Do You Understand That Margin Trading Amplifies Both the Profit and the Loss?

It's important to be aware that margin trading can work either in your favor or against you. Let's take an example to understand the benefits and the risks.

Let's assume that your broker allows you to trade with 1 percent margin. In your trading account, you have $20,000. XYZ is currently priced at $50. You make your research, and you conclude that XYZ may go up. You are pretty confident in your forecast, and you decide to buy two thousand XYZ at $50. This means that your exposure will be as follows: 2,000 XYZ × $50 = $100,000.

Because you trade with 1 percent margin, it's not necessary to have the entire amount of $100,000 in your trading account. To open your trade, you just need the following:

1% (the margin as percentage) × $100,000 (the value of the trade) = $1,000.

What happens if your forecast is correct and the price goes up 1 percent?

The new price for XYZ is $50 × 1.01 = $50.50.
Your profit for one XYZ is $50.50 − $50 = $0.50.
Your profit for two thousand XYZ is 2,000 × $0.50 = $1,000.

So if the price moves in your favor only 1 percent, you make a profit of $1,000, which means that you double your initial investment (the margin you had to use to place the trade).

What happens if the price has a 10 percent increase?

The new price for XYZ is $50 × 1.10 = $55.
Your profit for one XYZ is $55 − $50 = $5.

Your profit for two thousand XYZ is $2,000 \times \$5 = \$10,000$.

So if the price moves in your favor 10 percent, you make a profit of $10,000, which means that you multiply ten times your initial investment.

Are you excited? Don't be just yet. Let's see what happens if your forecast proves to be wrong.

If the price goes down 1 percent:
The new price for XYZ is $\$50 \times 0.99 = \$49.50$.
Your loss for one XYZ is $\$49.50 - \$50 = -\$0.50$.
Your loss for two thousand XYZ is $2,000 \times (-\$0.50) = -\$1,000$.

So if the price moves against you only 1 percent, you lose $1,000 (your entire initial investment).

If the price goes down 10 percent:
The new price for XYZ is $\$50 \times 0.90 = \$45$.
Your loss for one XYZ is $\$45 - \$50 = -\$5$.
Your loss for two thousand XYZ is $2,000 \times (-\$5) = -\$10,000$.

So if the price moves against you 10 percent, you lose $10,000 (ten times the initial investment).

As you can see, margin trading allows you to take much bigger exposures, compared to the amount of money you have in your trading account, which means that it significantly amplifies the potential profits or losses of your trades.

Well, what do you think about margin trading now?

#39 Avoid the Trap of Seeing the Glass Half Full

In general, being optimistic and focusing on the positive is not a bad thing. But when you trade on margin, it's important to be aware that it can work against you. You can end up losing a lot of money, in the blink of an eye.

Unfortunately there are traders who discover margin trading and choose to focus only on the positive and to ignore the huge risks. From "Margin trading can amplify both profits and losses," they choose to understand only that margin trading can help them obtain bigger profits.

From:

"If you trade with 1 percent margin, and the price moves as little as 1 percent, you can either double your initial investment or lose it entirely. If the price moves 10 percent, you can either win or lose ten times the initial investment."

they choose to hear:

"If you trade with 1 percent margin, and the price moves as little as 1 percent, you can double your initial investment. If the price moves 10 percent, you can win ten times the initial investment."

Margin trading is a double-edged sword. It can help professional and experienced traders obtain better results. For inexperienced traders, it can become a lethal weapon. Blinded by their own greed, they chase the jackpot, and they end up losing a lot of money.

#40 Don't Use Margin Trading to Place High-Risk Bets. Don't Trade like a Maniac

The "maniac trader" is actually a compulsive gambler. His trading activity has nothing to do with investments. For him, margin trading is a high-risk gamble. He hopes to clean up. Trading best practices, risk management, technical analysis, fundamental analysis, etc.—all these mean nothing to him. His view is easier and simpler: it's either up or down. The maniac trader/gambler has only two rules: (1) finding the lowest possible margin and (2) always going in with all his money.

Let's take an example. Let's assume that a maniac trader/gambler opens a trading account with 0.10 percent margin and deposits $3,000. He makes a quick calculation: if he goes in with all his money, he can take an exposure of $3 million.

$3,000,000 (total exposure) × 0.10% (margin) = $3,000 (blocked margin)

After that, he scans the market to find a ticker. One way or the other, he finds XYZ, and he places a trade for $3 million, blocking his entire amount of money ($3,000) as margin.

During the next few minutes or even seconds, the price moves 0.10 percent (either up or down). If he is lucky, and the price moves in his favor, he has a profit of $3,000. If fate is against him and the price moves against his bet, he loses the entire amount of $3,000[v].

Do you think he stands a chance in the long run?

#41 The Invisible Risk of Margin Trading

I am talking about the fact that margin trading exponentially increases the intensity of your emotions (the "good old friends" Fear and Greed), which makes it very hard to stay calm and take rational trading decisions.

Let's take an example. You consider that XYZ has the potential to go up around 5 percent during the next few trading sessions, and you have $10,000 available for this particular trade.

If you don't trade on margin, according to your forecast you can expect a profit of $500 ($10,000 × 5%).

If you trade with 1 percent margin and use the entire $10,000 as blocked margin, you can take an exposure of $1 million. This means that you can expect a potential profit of $50,000 ($1,000,000 × 5%).

The difference in profit between $500 and $50,000—*wow!* Faced with the possibility to win a bigger amount of money, your greed will be so much more intense, maybe even one hundred times more intense. It will be much harder to keep calm.

The feeling of fear is also exponentially amplified. Let's say that you normally handle pretty well a losing trade, as long as the loss is not bigger than $2,000. Once you see the loss exceeding $2,000, you lose your head.

If you don't trade on margin, the price has to decrease 20 percent in order for the loss to reach the psychological level of $2,000 ($10,000 × 20%).

If you trade with 1 percent margin, only a small pullback of just 0.20 percent is required for the loss to reach $2,000 ($1,000,000 × 0.20%).

Twenty percent versus 0.20 percent—the difference is, again, *wow!* That's why it's so much easier to panic when you trade on margin, maybe even one hundred times easier.

The bottom line: margin trading amplifies the emotions in the first place because each small price fluctuation—as little as 0.10 percent—can mean a significantly higher profit or loss, and it will be difficult to win the battles against greed and fear. You are only one step away from irrational decisions that can translate into a loss, an amplified loss.

Let's Draw Some Conclusions

If you don't have enough experience in trading…

If you don't have a solid risk management system, tested by time…

If you don't know yourself in terms of investment psychology…

…don't trade on margin with your money, at least not yet.

Test margin trading on a demo account. Take the necessary time to practice, to understand how it works, and to see how much risk you can handle; develop your risk management and trading strategies, test and improve them.

If you reach the conclusion that margin trading is too risky for you, that's great! Just stay away from it.

If you decide to try trading on margin with your own money, start small and see how it goes.

Don't forget: margin trading can be a deadly weapon in the wrong hands.

What Is Short Selling[vi]?

So far, we have discussed mainly about the concept of making profits by applying the rule: buy low and sell high, applicable when you expect the price to move up.

What happens if you forecast a decline in the price of a financial instrument you don't own?

Scenario 1: You wait.
If you are wrong, and the price goes up, you just lose an opportunity (because you didn't buy). If you are correct, and the price moves down, you wait, and you wait...until you identify the signals pointing that the downtrend may be over. Then it's time to apply the rule "buy low and sell high."

Scenario 2: You sell short.
Short selling is the operation of selling a financial instrument you don't own, and repurchasing it at a later date. The goal is to profit from the falling prices, by applying the rule: "sell high and buy low."

If you anticipate the price to slide, you sell short. If your forecast is correct, and the price dips, you buy later at a lower price, and make a profit. If your prediction is wrong and the price goes up, you lose because you buy at a higher price.

Let's take an example.

XYZ is traded at $10. You don't have any open positions on XYZ. You have a pessimistic view on XYZ, and you decide to sell short five hundred XYZ at $10 each. Your exposure is: 500 XYZ × $10 = $5,000; this is a short position.

If you are right, and the price moves down to $8.50, you can close your short position buying five hundred XYZ at $8.50

each. By selling at \$10.00 and buying afterward at \$8.50, you record a profit of: 500 × (\$10.00 − \$8.50) = \$750.

If your forecast proves to be incorrect, and the price goes up to \$10.50, you close your position buying five hundred XYZ at \$10.50 each. By selling at \$10.00 each and buying later at \$10.50 each, you record a loss of: 500 × (\$10.00 − \$10.50) = −\$250.

#42 "You Can Win When Prices Fall" versus "There Is a Higher Probability to Lose If Your Forecasts Are Incorrect"

Many traders are excited when they discover short selling. Until then, they only had the possibility to profit from rising prices. Now they have unlimited opportunities to make money, as they can speculate falling prices as well.

This view is correct. But something is missing—a big "if." You can make money from both rising and falling prices, "if" your forecast is correct. Otherwise, you lose.

For experienced traders, short selling offers indeed more opportunities. The story may be different for inexperienced traders because trading becomes more difficult.

When you have more chances to win ("if" your forecast is correct), you are more willing to take risks and trade more. You can bet on both a rising and a falling price.

What if you buy and the price slides? No problem. You close your long position with a loss, and you sell short, hoping that the price will continue to go down. If it seems that the downtrend is actually over, and the price recovers, again, no problem. You close your short position, generating another loss, and soon after that, you buy again, hoping that this time your bet will pay off. And repeat this cycle.

The roller coaster is already moving too fast for a beginner. Both margin trading and short selling significantly increase its speed. You need to be careful and act smart; otherwise you may end up being thrown to the ground and may lose your hard-earned money.

Part 14: Key Takeaways

Key Takeaways

#1# Trading and investing are two different things.

When you trade, you try to speculate the short-term price fluctuations. You place frequent trades, keeping your open positions for minutes, hours, days, or even weeks. Investing involves fewer trades and a "buy and hold" approach. An investor keeps his or her open positions for months or even years.

A trader's goal is to get higher returns than an investor does.

#2# Trading is hard.

Opening a trading account and placing trades is simple. Anyone can do this. Becoming a profitable trader and managing to be consistent in the long run—well, this is the challenge. And not everybody can do it.

#3# Trading is risky.

You can lose money, even the entire amount you have in your trading account. You just have to understand and accept this possibility before you decide to start trading.

#4# Trading requires strong knowledge, practice, experience, self-discipline, and time.

If you don't have a background in finance or investing, don't rush. Before placing your first trade on the market, you need to learn. It may take hundreds of hours, if not thousands, to build your know-how about fundamental and technical analysis, risk management, and investment psychology and to practice on a demo account and develop and test your strategies.

You have to be willing to spend the necessary time and to accumulate knowledge and experience. Remember, your money is at stake.

#5# Trading may not be suitable for you.

How do you feel about losing? I know that you hate the idea; who doesn't? But how do you cope with it? If only the thought of losing money makes you panic, you have to consider that trading may not be suitable for you.

Also, if you don't have the proper knowledge and experience and you are not willing to spend hundreds and hundreds of hours to learn, you will end up gambling instead of trading. So you should stay away from it.

#6# Managing your emotions is one of the essential factors that can make the difference between success and failure.

You may have very solid knowledge about trading, market analysis, and risk management, but it's not enough because when our emotions run high, our logic runs low. That's a fact.

If you are not able to maintain your rational thinking in times of stress, it will be difficult for you to properly implement in practice all the theoretical things that you know.

Trading the markets means either winning or losing money. That's why fear and greed often kick in. When that happens, most of us stop thinking rationally. We act rashly and make irrational decisions, which lead to bad trades and losses.

#7# There are no guarantees for success.

You need to be aware that no matter how hard you work and how much you learn and practice, you may not become a profitable trader in the long run. You may have better chances if you put in more time and effort, but there are no guarantees that you will not end up losing money.

#8# Understand the opportunity cost.

Trading involves investing both your money and your time. You hope for a nice positive return, but as we already discussed, there are no guarantees. This means that in the long run, you may end up losing, or winning an insignificant amount of money.

Your opportunity cost is related to all the hours you have spent on trading. You could have chosen to do a lot of other things, such as boosting your professional career, spending time with your family, and pursuing your passions and hobbies. All these could have led to a higher quality of life. That's your opportunity cost right there!

To better understand, let's take an example. Bob started trading five years ago. He initially spent around 540 hours to learn about trading (on average, three hours per day, for six months). During the next four years and a half, he allocated around 1,620 hours for reading the news, making his research, and placing the trades (on average, one hour per day for four and a half years). After five years of trading, he has a total profit of $4,000. Bob is glad that he did not lose, but he is somehow disappointed: he invested more than twenty-one hundred hours. So basically he won less than two dollars per hour. He could have used his time to focus his efforts on his professional career, and that could have helped him achieve promotions and better salaries. He could have spent time with his wife and kids to improve his relationship with them; he could have learned to play the guitar (he always wished that!). He could have done a lot of other things. All these are opportunity costs.

This is not something specific to trading. It's actually a rule of life: whenever we choose to do something, we actually choose not to do some other thing.

#9# Do *not*

...trade with money you can't afford to lose;

...gamble with financial products; or

...let yourself become addicted to trading.

#10# Develop your trading plan and your risk management system.

Don't trade randomly. Create clear rules for the following factors:

+ what elements you take into account to support your trading decision

+ how you decide what to buy/sell and when to do it

+ how much you are willing to risk in one particular trade

+ how you estimate where to place your stop-loss and take-profit orders

+ what risk-reward ratio you are looking for in a trade

+ etc.

#11# Don't place a trade just because your intuition pushes you to do it.

Intuition is defined as the ability to understand something instinctively, without the need for conscious reasoning. The brain uses our past experiences to create patterns. In a particular situation when a decision may be needed, the brain extracts the information available at that time and tries to determine which pattern better fits that particular situation. After identifying and selecting a pattern, it creates a response. That's when we have (feel) an intuition that we should act in a specific manner.

The problem is that the brain does not always identify the correct patterns. Sure, we know we should not touch a hot stove, but this is an easy pattern. When the pattern is more complex and it's necessary to put together a lot of pieces of information, it's harder to identify the correct pattern. That's why sometimes, our intuition proves to be correct, and sometimes it proves to be wrong.

Don't trade solely on your intuition. Slow down and examine your assumptions. And don't forget about your trading-plan rules.

#12# Three things you should not forget:

#12.1 When the market proves you wrong, reassess your trade. If necessary, don't be afraid to cut your losses. Don't just hope that the market will recover.

#12.2 A profit is locked in only when you close your winning trade.

#12.3 Properly timing your trades is essential. You may accurately forecast the market direction, but if your timing is not good (i.e., the timing when you open or close the trade), you may still suffer a loss. This doesn't mean that you have to buy the lows and sell the highs.

#13# Don't overtrade.

Placing a lot of trades in a short period of time means a higher cost with the commissions and fees paid to your broker. Usually overtrading makes (a lot of) money, not for you but for your broker.

#14# There is no one-size-fits-all approach.

What works for one trader may not work for another one. There is no magic set of rules that automatically transforms you into a profitable trader. It's up to each trader to build his own trading systems and risk management strategies. You can learn from other people's experiences, but you have to filter everything through your own thinking process.

At the end of the day, you, and only you, are responsible for your money, your trading decisions, and the results you get, either profits or losses.

A Few Final Thoughts

Like hundreds and thousands of individual traders who start trading each day, I was also full of hope and enthusiasm when I placed my first trade on the market. Today I see trading with new eyes, because during the past eleven years, I made mistakes, and I have learned a lot.

I hope that the information I presented will prove to be useful for you. I hope that now you understand better how trading may look and feel like. I hope that you are more aware of the possible risks and mistakes associated with trading.

You may not agree with all the ideas, and that's fine. There is no Holy Grail in trading, and I certainly did not intend to create one through this miniguide. In fact, I encourage you to filter everything through your own thinking process.

Before saying good-bye, please let me share with you how I see trading now:

I am much more cautious.

I trade with a small part of my savings.

I trade only those financial instruments whose level of risk I am comfortable with.

I understand that having a day job (that it's not related to trading) makes trading more difficult, at least short-term trading. That's why I now prefer trading on longer time frames.

My goal is no longer to become a market millionaire. I am searching for positive returns, and the profits (in absolute values) have to justify all the hours I spend with researching the market and trading.

\# Last but not least, I no longer feel the craving to trade, no matter what. If I don't find a trading opportunity with solid arguments, or if I just don't have the time to monitor the markets, I choose not to trade.

In the end, I would like to thank you for buying and reading this miniguide. **Please let me know your opinion on the book by providing your review.**

Wishing you all the best!
Andrei Puscaragiu

PS—If you found this book useful, please recommend it to your friends who may be interested in it.

Notes

[i] When the price reaches the stop-loss level set by the trader, the stop-loss order becomes active and the open position is closed at the current market price, which may be different than the stop-loss level. In order to understand the characteristics of the stop-loss order, please discuss with your broker.

[ii] When the price reaches the stop-loss level set by the trader, the stop-loss order becomes active and the open position is closed at the current market price, which may be different than the stop-loss level. In this particular example, if the open position is closed at a price different than the stop-loss level, then the value of the loss may exceed $500. In order to understand the characteristics of the stop-loss order, please discuss with your broker.

[iii] When the price reaches the take-profit level set by the trader, the take-profit order becomes active and the open position is closed at the current market price, which may be different than the take-profit level. In order to understand the characteristics of the take-profit order, please discuss with your broker.

[iv] Margin trading is extremely risky and you can lose more than your initial investment. Margin trading can incur additional trading costs. In order to understand the characteristics of margin trading, please discuss with your broker.

[v] Margin trading is extremely risky and you can lose more than your initial investment. In order to understand the characteristics of margin trading, please discuss with your broker.

[vi] The technical mechanism, fees, commissions, and any other costs related to short selling can be different based on factors such as: the market or exchange where you trade, the broker you choose to trade with, the financial instrument, etc. To understand the characteristics of short selling, please discuss with your broker.

Made in the USA
Middletown, DE
09 January 2017